FONZ & GAMES
"People would dream about doing the things the Fonz was doing," says Winkler, who has become a TV producer as well as an actor, "and I was living off his reputation."

Ayyyy! List

The man who gave us **the Fonz** fondly recalls the innovations and excesses of the great, goofy decade that made him so famous he wanted to hide in his apartment.

BY HENRY WINKLER

I never had a **Pet Rock** until recently. I never quite made it to Studio 54. I never got into disco clothes. **Leisure suits?** As a matter of fact, I thought polyester caused rashes. For me the '70s began with a stomach ache, when I graduated from the Yale School of Drama in 1970 worried about my future. I thought, "Now what am I going to do?"

SYLVESTER STALLONE was a friend of mine. He had such a

I joined the Yale Repertory Theatre, then left Yale and did more theater in Washington, D.C. I was making $185 a week—a fortune. I finally had enough money to buy the first overcoat that could keep me warm in winter. But after three weeks I was fired. I'd like to think it was because the director always had another actor in mind, someone who wasn't available at first. So I was just filling space.

I headed for New York, where I started doing commercials. My first was for **Close-Up tooth-paste.** At the same time, the Boeing 747 was introduced. I remember thinking, "Wow. Big plane." But it wasn't until I was earning a living and could afford to go to Europe that I really appreciated this steel giant that could fly 400 people across the ocean.

The invention I truly appreciated at the time was **the pocket calculator,** also introduced in 1970. Being in the bottom three percent of the country in math, I'm personally grateful for the pocket calculator. All of a sudden there was this thing I could put a battery in and let it do the figuring for me. I would go to the market and use it to find out if I was getting the right change.

I was very nervous about going to Hollywood, where people were at least three and a half inches taller than me. But I went. I landed in Los Angeles on September 18, 1973, at 2:45 p.m. About a month later, I auditioned for *Happy Days.*

I went in with very long hair and a gigantic sweat stain under my armpit. I thought honesty was the best policy, so I pointed to my right armpit and said, "This is in direct correlation to the fear that is running through my body." I know they were looking for tall and muscular, so I put height and muscles in my voice. Thank God, they saw them. **Sylvester Stallone** was a friend of mine. He had such a powerful personality. I thought, "What would Sly do here?"

I was called in for a second audition. This time I had my hair cut, and the producers combed it into a D.A. They took my unibrow and made two of them. I spent the afternoon having the middle of my eyebrow plucked. I was red and irritated when I went in to audition for Barry Diller, who was then with ABC.

On my birthday—October 30—I got the call. "Would you like to play Fonzie?"

It was very exciting and scary. I said okay.

FONZIE & BEYOND

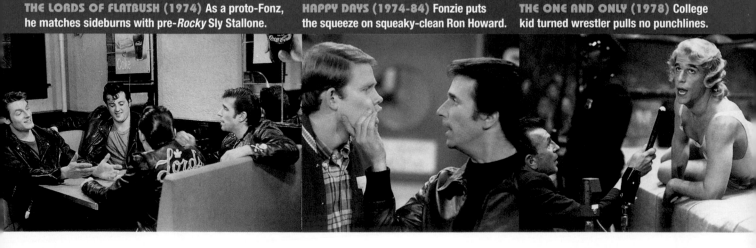

THE LORDS OF FLATBUSH (1974) As a proto-Fonz, he matches sideburns with pre-*Rocky* Sly Stallone.

HAPPY DAYS (1974-84) Fonzie puts the squeeze on squeaky-clean Ron Howard.

THE ONE AND ONLY (1978) College kid turned wrestler pulls no punchlines.

powerful personality. I thought, "What would Sly do here?"

This was around the time of the **oil crisis.** People were on line all over the country trying to get gas. Instead of going on vacation, people pitched tents in their backyards.

I was the seventh character on the show. I only worked one day a week, and got paid $1000 for that one day. Suddenly I could eat three times a day. I got a one-bedroom apartment on Laurel Avenue, across from where the Virgin Megastore is now on Sunset Boulevard in West Hollywood. The apartment had a kitchenette and wet bar. I didn't drink, but I bought Almaden wine—I had a jug of red and a jug of white for when friends stopped by. I always had a tuna sandwich from Greenblatt's Deli up the street. Dan Fogelberg was always on my record player. And I had five plants.

We did a show where Fonzie drops back into school and has to take a test. He wants to cheat, but various events won't allow him to. He ends up passing anyway. That was the first episode that featured The Fonz.

Suddenly Fonzie started to grow. I was asked to make a personal appearance at a mall in Little Rock, Arkansas. I arrived at 11:30 p.m. There were about 3000 people in the terminal, screaming and yelling, all dressed in '50s outfits. I got back on the plane because I thought I had walked into somebody's party. They said, "No, this is all for you."

I walked through the airport in shock, just saying hello to everybody. There was this one girl who literally attached herself to me, like jewelry. I was carrying my bags and at the same time carrying her through this gauntlet of people. Finally I said, "Do you think you should get off now?" And she said, "I'll never have this opportunity again, so I don't think so."

One is not born with the ability to handle celebritydom. How did I handle it? I stayed in my apartment for a very long time. I had my fan mail delivered there, and read it, and tried to answer some of it. That way I felt I had a task. I was being productive and I never had to leave my apartment.

Of course, I'd go to movies. I nearly gave up acting after I saw Martin Scorsese's *Mean Streets*, with Robert DeNiro and Harvey Keitel. Those guys were unbelievable. I didn't know if I could reach that level.

Great movies came out in the '70s: *The French Connection, The Godfather, The Sting, One Flew Over the Cuckoo's Nest, The Deer Hunter, Rocky.* And of course there was **Jaws,** which changed everyone's attitude towards swimming. *Saturday Night*

When **ROBIN WILLIAMS** first appeared as **MORK** on **HAPPY DAYS,** my entire job was to keep a straight face

Fever was a lot of fun, but I didn't get into the disco thing. I once went to a big disco in Manhattan called Arthur, but it made me too nervous. You couldn't hear anyone speak.

The Bee Gees still transport me back to the '70s. People who are that successful are successful for a reason. They had one great song after another. There was also Crosby, Stills, Nash and Young. Those guys kept reinventing themselves. I loved the sound of Kim Carnes' voice. "Bette Davis Eyes," which came out just after the '70s, was fabulous.

Robin Williams and Steve Martin were geniuses of the '70s. When Robin first appeared as **Mork** on *Happy Days,* my entire job, almost impossible, was to keep a straight face. He was this very shy, quiet, reserved man. Then he lit into the script and you never saw anything like it. It was astounding. Steve Martin was equally brilliant. When he was

doing one of his Tut concerts he asked me to come out—just walk on and off the stage—while he was singing "King Tut." Having him ask me to do that walk-on was one of the great compliments I got in my life.

When I met Stacey, my future wife, she loved **Boz Scaggs.** One of the first things she introduced me to was his music. She also had a son, Jed, who was a huge Kiss fan. He was six years old, and we would go out and get makeup. I would do his face like Kiss. Then he would jump on his bed and play his miniature guitar.

Jed also had his Big Wheels—these oversize colorful plastic tricycles that were really popular then. I had a **beanbag chair.** It was one of my first pieces of furniture. It was very comfortable for a while, but then you would sort of crush the little balls inside and the chair wasn't so comfortable.

Not long ago I started carrying a little pet rock in my pocket. I really began to understand how you can grow attached to an inanimate object. It follows you around wherever you go. I finally put mine back in the garden, where he came from. He wasn't store bought. He was a natural guy. Sometimes you just have to go, "Wow. America. Is this a great country or what?" Soon they're going to sell pieces of wood, so you can have them to knock on.

The most important event of the '70s for me was marrying Stacey and having Jed come into my life. We were married on May 5, 1978, in New York, in the synagogue where I had been bar mitzvahed. Marriage grounds you. It gives you the ability to balance all the other stuff, because the other stuff can grind you down.

The '70s and *Happy Days* will always be with me. People still come up to me and say, "I grew up with you. I named my animal after you. I loved you. I learned to speak English by watching you." I was only this actor playing The Fonz. Certainly I could never be this guy, this wonderful figment of our wildest imaginations. That's why I'd have to say to people, "Excuse me, I'm Henry Winkler." Because off-camera I couldn't even try to be him. Although once, like the Fonz, I did try to smack the side of my apartment building and make all the lights inside go on.

It didn't work.

ABOVE: In 1978, newlyweds Henry and Stacey and her son Jed quickly bonded as a family.
RIGHT: Winkler earned his pave rave in 1981.

BELOW: Henry, with his and Stacey's son, Max, helped serve Thanksgiving Dinner to the homeless in 1999.

WALK OF FAME

HENRY WINKLER

LOS ANGELES MISSION

LOS ANGELES MISSION

People weekly

CELEBRATES THE 70s

BELLE ON WHEELS: OLIVIA NEWTON-JOHN GOT PHYSICAL IN 1979

STAFF FOR THIS BOOK

EDITOR: Eric Levin
EXECUTIVE EDITOR: Kelly Knauer
ART DIRECTOR: Anthony Wing Kosner
PICTURE EDITOR: Patricia Cadley
CONTRIBUTING WRITERS: Connie Dickerson
Mark Gauthier, Jon Young
CHIEF OF REPORTERS: Deirdre van Dyk
CHIEF OF RESEARCH: Denise Lynch
RESEARCH ASSOCIATE: Lela Nargi
DESIGNER: Scott G. Weiss
COPY EDITOR: Bruce Christopher Carr

Special thanks to: Victor Baez, Richard Burgheim, Brien Foy, Penny Hays, Evie McKenna, Gregory Monfries, Jason Lancaster, Gregory Monfries, Stephen Pabarue

Copyright ©2000 Time Inc. Home Entertainment
Published by

People Books ®

A division of Time Inc. Home Entertainment
1271 Avenue of the Americas
New York, NY 10020

PRESIDENT: Stuart Hotchkiss
EXECUTIVE DIRECTOR, BRANDED BUSINESSES: David Arfine
EXECUTIVE DIRECTOR, NON-BRANDED BUSINESSES: Alicia Longobardo
EXECUTIVE DIRECTOR, TIME INC. BRAND LICENSING: Risa Turken
DIRECTOR, LICENSING: Scott Rosenzweig
DIRECTOR, MARKETING SERVICES: Michael Barrett
DIRECTOR, RETAIL & SPECIAL SALES: Tom Mifsud
DIRECTOR, BRANDED BUSINESSES: Maarten Terry
ASSOCIATE DIRECTORS: Roberta Harris, Kenneth Maehlum
PRODUCT MANAGERS: Dana Gregory, Andre Okolowitz, Ann Marie Ross, Niki Viswanathan, Daria Raehse
ASSOCIATE PRODUCT MANAGERS: Victoria Alfonso, Jennifer Dowell, Dennis Sheehan, Meredith Shelley, Lauren Zaslansky
ASSISTANT PRODUCT MANAGERS: Ann Gillespie, Virginia Valdes
MANAGER, MARKETING SERVICES: Marina Weinstein
ASSOCIATE MANAGER, MARKETING SERVICES E-COMMERCE: Dima Masrizada
LICENSING MANAGER: Joanna West
ASSOCIATE LICENSING MANAGER: Regina Feiler
LICENSING COORDINATOR: Laury Shapiro
ASSOCIATE MANAGER, RETAIL & NEW MARKETS: Bozena Szwagulinski
EDITORIAL OPERATIONS DIRECTOR: John Calvano
ASSISTANT EDITORIAL OPERATIONS MANAGER: Emily Rabin
BOOK PRODUCTION MANAGER: Jessica McGrath
ASSOCIATE BOOK PRODUCTION MANAGER: Jonathan Polsky
ASSISTANT BOOK PRODUCTION MANAGER: Suzanne DeBenedetto
FULFILLMENT MANAGER: Richard Perez
ASSISTANT FULFILLMENT MANAGER: Tara Schimming
FINANCIAL DIRECTOR: Tricia Griffin
FINANCIAL MANAGER: Robert Dente
ASSOCIATE FINANCIAL MANAGER: Steven Sandonato
ASSISTANT FINANCIAL MANAGER: Tamara Whittier
EXECUTIVE ASSISTANT: Mary Jane Rigoroso

HARDCOVER ISBN: 1-883013-99-2
Library of Congress Catalog Number: 00-101240

We welcome your comments and suggestions about PEOPLE Books.
Please write to us at:

PEOPLE Books
Attention: Book Editors
P.O. Box 11016
Des Moines, IA 50336-1016

If you would like to order any of our Hard Cover Collector's Edition books, please call us at 1-800-327-6388, Monday through Friday, 7:00 a.m.–8:00 p.m., or Saturday, 7:00 a.m.–6:00p.m., Central Time.

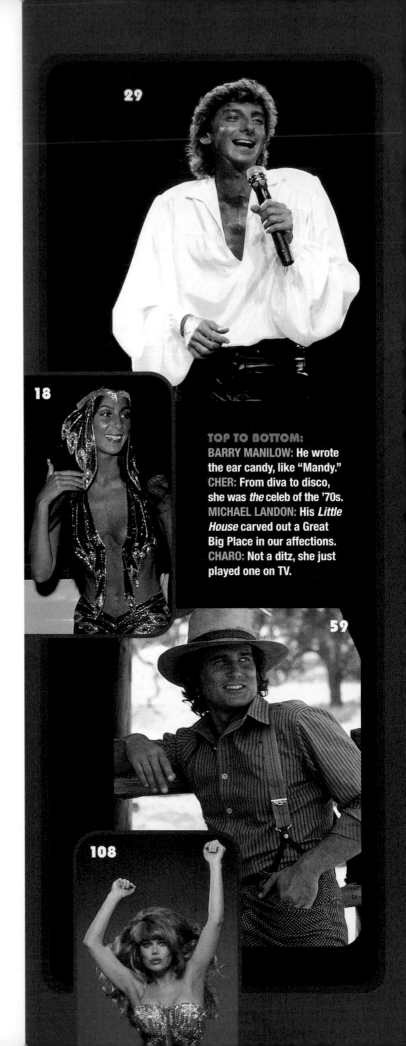

TOP TO BOTTOM:
BARRY MANILOW: He wrote the ear candy, like "Mandy."
CHER: From diva to disco, she was *the* celeb of the '70s.
MICHAEL LANDON: His *Little House* carved out a Great Big Place in our affections.
CHARO: Not a ditz, she just played one on TV.

CONTENTS

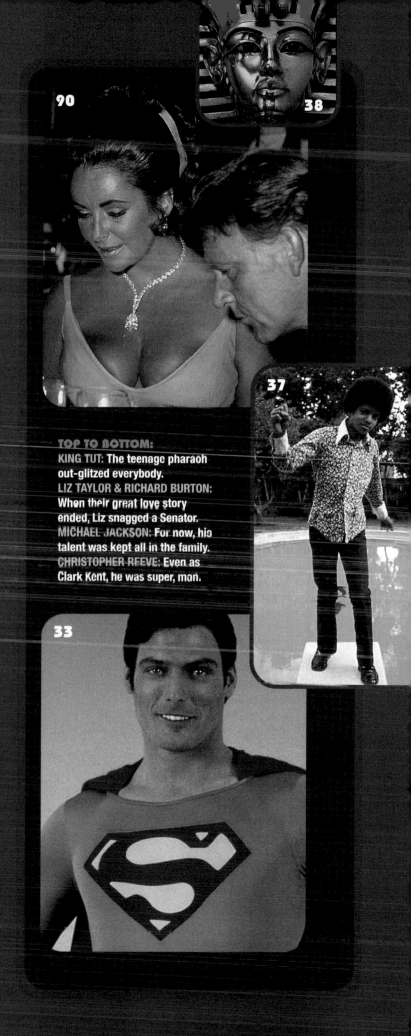

90   38

37

33

TOP TO BOTTOM:
KING TUT: The teenage pharaoh
out-glitzed everybody.
LIZ TAYLOR & RICHARD BURTON:
When their great love story
ended, Liz snagged a Senator.
MICHAEL JACKSON: For now, his
talent was kept all in the family.
CHRISTOPHER REEVE: Even as
Clark Kent, he was super, man.

THE WAY WE WERE

Memories ... were we really
so innocent then? Or has time
simply scrambled our brain cells?

Long ago, and oh so far away ...

We jogged our way toward perfection

PACE-SETTERS
Farrah Fawcett-Majors—whose "wings" were the 'do of the decade—got in shape with hubby Lee Majors, star of ABC's *The Six Million Dollar Man.* Their glamorous marriage ended with the decade, in 1980.

... While some let the good times roll

ROLLER GIRL
In the Me Decade, we ran, we rolled, we fasted, we Ested. And we yearned for the beauty and energy of youth—as epitomized by Brooke Shields, 14, skating in New York City's Central Park in 1979.

We dreamed of being the ideal family

MARCIA, MARCIA ...
If you grew up in the '70s—hey, you're an honorary Brady! Then again, if you've grown up in the U.S.A. anytime *since* the '70s—you're an honorary Brady. For though *The Brady Bunch* only ran from 1969 to 1974, the re-runs haven't stopped.

... And learned to live with the reality

TRUTH SERUM
Silly, shaggy and subversive, producer Norman Lear's *All in the Family*, debuting in '71, made us face our prejudices—and laugh at them—thanks to Sally Struthers, Rob Reiner, Jean Stapleton and Carroll O'Connor.

At night we whirled to a disco beat

SHAKE YOUR BOOTY

We may not have known it, but we were starving for a chance to get out on the floor and gyrate to a pounding, numbing, repetitive thump. So when *Saturday Night Fever* hit the big screen in 1977 and the Bee Gees sang, "You should be dancin'," we joined in for the chorus: "Yeah!"

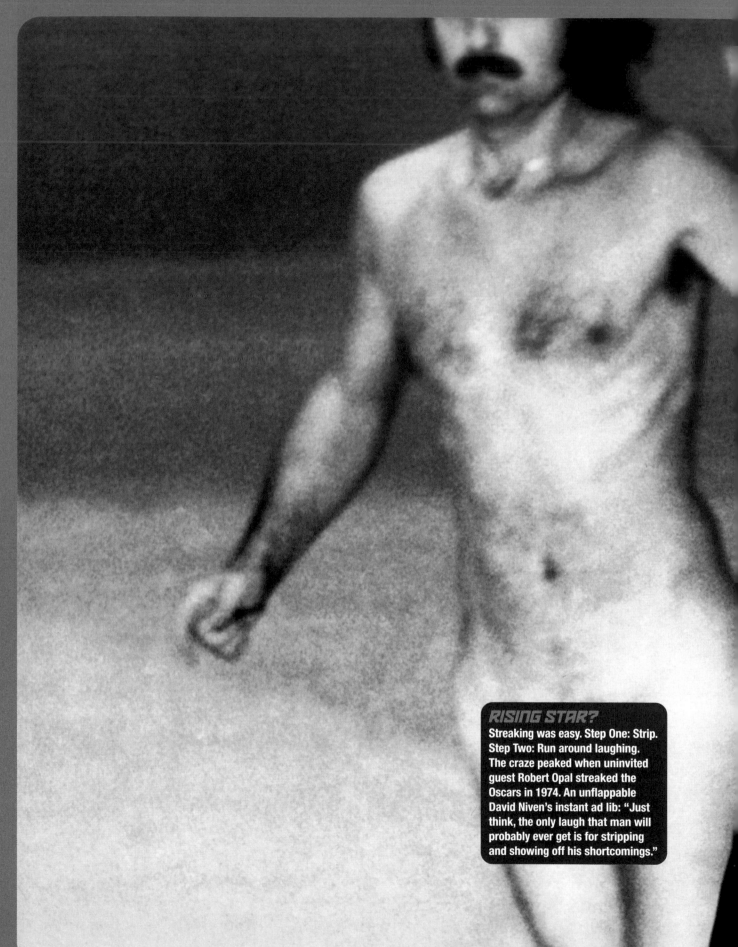

RISING STAR?

Streaking was easy. Step One: Strip. Step Two: Run around laughing. The craze peaked when uninvited guest Robert Opal streaked the Oscars in 1974. An unflappable David Niven's instant ad lib: "Just think, the only laugh that man will probably ever get is for stripping and showing off his shortcomings."

THE ME DECADE 🙂

JANEFONDA

From "Hanoi Jane" to fitness guru, she marched to her own drummer

THE VASSAR-EDUCATED daughter of Hollywood royalty (Henry Fonda), Jane was a living seismograph of the times. Her quest for identity found her morphing from Hollywood ingenue (*Barefoot in the Park)* to titillating space goddess (*Barbarella)* to Serious Actress *(They Shoot Horses, Don't They?)*. The 1970s brought us Vietnam activist Jane, progressive-democratic house-wife Jane and Oscar-winning Jane—the Academy lauded her fine perfor-mances in *Klute* (1971) and *Coming Home* (1978). So who was surprised when the 1979 opening of the her workout studio in Beverly Hills gave us ... Jumpin' Jane? Fonda's workout books and videos made her the queen of female fitness. Those were the highs. The lows? Twenty-three "agonizing" years of bulimia. Condemnation by veterans and members of Congress for treasonable actions in her days as the enemy-turf-trodding "Hanoi Jane"; and failed marriages to French film director Roger Vadim (divorced amicably, 1968) and California politician Tom Hayden (divorced mud-slingingly, 1990). Her quest for fulfillment goes on: In 2000 she split from tycoon Ted Turner.

GO FOR THE BURN Applying the same zeal with which she had attacked film and politics, Fonda became the poster gal for the millions of women who shared her zest for getting into shape. By 1986, *Jane Fonda's Workout Book* would sell some 2 million copies.

JOHNLENNON

Fleeing the flashbulbs, he gave peace a chance

AS THE DECADE THEY helped define came to an end, so did the Beatles: They split up forever in the spring of 1970. For John Lennon, often considered the leader of the group, the breakup promised an opportunity to explore new directions. The next few years found him bouncing like a pinball from public concerns (with radical-politics songs like "Power to the People") to the private explorations more typical of the new decade (after taking trendy primal scream therapy with Yoko, he wrote deeply personal songs like "Mother"). In 1971, just as John released his fine solo album, *Imagine*—featuring its uplifting, utopian title cut—he and Yoko moved to New York City to begin a new life. But John was distracted by legal battles with U.S. immigration authorities, who sought to deport him because of a 1968 pot bust and his suspect politics. Suddenly, John seemed to lose his way. From October 1973 to March 1975, he left Yoko to indulge in a "lost weekend" that found him abusing drugs and drink with an L.A. party crowd.

But John returned to Yoko, and after their son Sean was born in October 1975, Lennon found a new identity: househusband. While Yoko ran their business affairs, John retreated to the couple's digs in New York City's famed Dakota apartment house, living in near-total seclusion. Tragically, just as John had begun an artistic comeback with the album *Double Fantasy,* in December, 1980, he was shot and killed by a crazed stalker, Mark David Chapman. John's quiet years—and the '70s—were over.

BETTYFORD

She pioneered inner space by going public with her problems

SHE WAS ALWAYS ON THE MOVE: Betty Bloomer went from Grand Rapids gal to Bennington College student to Martha Graham dancer before meeting young Gerald Ford, a former University of Michigan football hero and soon to be a congressional candidate. When her Vice President husband assumed the Presidency in 1974 upon Richard Nixon's resignation, Betty was cast into the national spotlight. In her new role, she won America's respect—and led the march in the decade's new frankness about personal concerns—by unashamedly going public with private calamities that society had scrupulously hushed up for decades. In her initial year as First Lady, she disclosed that she would undergo a radical mastectomy: Her courage in openly discussing a formerly taboo topic dragged breast cancer out of the closet forever. She proved equally candid and pioneering about her struggles with alcohol and drug dependency, from which she began her recovery in 1978. She went on to help establish the Betty Ford Center for the treatment of addiction in Rancho Mirage, Calif., in 1982. Facing her battles with dignity and courage, and scouring the taint of outdated shame from personal health problems, this gutsy First Lady did every American a favor.

HAPPY TRIO John proudly held son Sean in 1975. For Lennon, who admitted he was a poor father to his son Julian (by first wife Cynthia), Sean's birth proved a turning point.

GET WELL SOON! The President and First Lady enjoyed a card bearing the best wishes of all 100 U.S. Senators after her surgery in 1974.

YOU'VE GOT A FRIEND

In the '60s we rocked out to groups. Now we searched for meaning with soulful soloists

CAROLE KING

A PIANO PLAYER at age 4, King broke into the biz at 16 as the Barbie of the Brill Building, the songwriter partner of soon-to-be-husband Gerry Goffin. The pair's chart toppers included "Up on the Roof" (for the Drifters), "One Fine Day" (for the Chiffons) and "The Loco-Motion" (for Little Eva, who was Carole's babysitter). But in the '70s, King stepped out from behind the curtain to create her own sound. Her *Tapestry* album in 1971 was a milestone: Embraced by fans, it sparked a cavalcade of copycats. One of the best-selling albums ever, it still sounds great.

JAMES TAYLOR

AN ADOLESCENCE OF institutionalization and depression didn't bode well. But North Carolinian Taylor stayed the course, and in 1971 "You've Got a Friend" reached No. 1. His marriage to chanteuse Carly Simon in 1973—they split up at the decade's end—helped seal his pedigree as musical royalty. "Fire and Rain" (1970) still makes boomers cry, and his concerts still sell out—maybe because he never did.

ROBERTA FLACK

A GUEST SHOT on a 1970 Bill Cosby TV special captivated viewers, and her career soared when first-time director Clint Eastwood used one of her songs in his 1971 stalker movie *Play Misty for Me.* When audiences heard Flack's restrained, hymn-like "The First Time Ever I Saw Your Face," they wanted more. The church organist's daughter, who went to Howard University on a music scholarship at 15, obliged. Fans loved "Killing Me Softly with His Song" (1973), her cover of a tune written about singer Don McLean—and later a '90s hit for the Fugees.

JONI MITCHELL

A PRODUCT OF THE Canadian prairies (by way of New York City and Malibu), the former Roberta Joan Anderson combined jazz-inflected melodies, poetic lyrics and a bell-clear soprano. The autobiographical heartbreak of *Blue* (1971), the free-wheeling pop of *Court and Spark* (1974) and the sonic experimentation of *Hejira* (1976) have in common sophistication, intelligence and personal insight.

CARLY SIMON

YOU'RE SO VAIN? Not really. It was stage fright that often plagued the career of this child of privilege. But recording? No problem. A Manhattan–and–Martha's Vineyard girlhood as the daughter of publishing tycoon Richard Simon (Simon & Schuster) gave way to icon status—thanks to songs like "Anticipation" and "Mockingbird"—as one the most potent voices in '70s pop-rock.

THESELLERSOFSELF

"Show me the way," Peter Frampton sang, and these celebrity pathfinders did the job

JULIACHILD

AN ECCENTRIC MANNER, an unrestrained ebullience in the kitchen (fed, viewers sometimes suspected, by an occasional nip from the cooking sherry) and a sometimes hilarious, singsong delivery didn't stop this Pasadena-born, self-described "hayseed" from becoming the doyenne of classic French cooking—for Americans. And why not? Her unpretentious embrace of haute cuisine and cordon bleu techniques (courtesy of her marriage to career diplomat Paul Child), and her no-nonsense "you can do it" attitude, brought crêpes and soufflés to millions of happy PBS viewers. The best news: Now in her late 80s, she's still cookin'.

WERNERERHARD

HE DIDN'T KNOW JACK? In fact, he buried him. Jack Rosenberg, a onetime construction supervisor from Pennsylvania, reinvented himself as Werner Erhard and offered a nation seeking personal fulfillment (but bored with transcendental meditation and Zen) his own brand of "religion": Erhard Seminars Training, or est. Americans flocked to Erhard's sessions, offbeat combinations of group encounter, bladder control training and spiritual epiphany. Today, he has left the U.S.; his whereabouts are unknown.

TOM WOLFE

HE'S KNOWN TODAY as a novelist *(Bonfire of the Vanities, A Man In Full,)* and white-suited boulevardier. But in a landmark 1976 magazine article, this pioneer of "new journalism" reported Americans' sudden interest in Eastern religions, health foods, feel-good fads, self-help books and cults. Describing our obsession with "remaking, remodeling, elevating, and polishing one's very self," he coined the term that forever pinned a butterfly era into place: "The Me Decade."

JIM FIXX

A RUNAWAY BESTSELLER? You bet. The force behind *The Complete Book of Running* (1977) was a formerly out-of-shape LIFE magazine editor, Jim Fixx. His anecdotal tale of slimming down and firming up boosted the popularity of jogging, while loping to No. 1 on the New York *Times* list, where it remained through numerous printings. Ironically, the man who had made his name synonymous with "running for your life" died in 1984 from a heart attack—in mid-stride.

THE LOUDS

MEET *REAL LIFE'S* DAD: Anthropologist Margaret Mead called the 1973 PBS documentary series *An American Family* "important as the invention of drama or the novel." Fans of the addictive "TV-vérité" event were treated to parents' Pat and Bill's divorce, gay son Lance's coming out, and other travails. Eleven million viewers watched, riveted.

Singular Sensations

There have always been stars. But the '70s bred **superstars** whose lives were just as flamboyant as their wardrobes

CHER

Flashy, trashy and fun, she rode fame's roller-coaster in high style

If you don't get Cher, you don't get the '70s. For Cher *was* the '70s, in all their over-the-top, over-the-edge, over-whatever-you've-got glory. A has-been when the decade began, she would end it in another career swoon. She would have plenty of comebacks left, including an Oscar for *Moonstruck* in 1987. But from 1970 to 1980 she took

LOVE CHILD Cher in the early '70s. She grew up fast: married to Sonny at 17, she was a star at 19 and over the hill at 23.

her wildest ride. Cher's periodic trips to the top have always been sweeter for the depths from which she's emerged. In the '70s, she weathered both—plus a lot of stops on the way. Like so many women of that restless era, she underwent wrenching life passages—divorce, motherhood, love affairs, career troubles, identity crises. Only she played them out in Technicolor for all to see, exposing (and exploiting) her personal life with the same insouciant charm with which she bared her lithe frame in a cavalcade of wacky, top-this outfits by Bob Mackie.

At the decade's beginning, Cherilyn Sarkisian Bono, 23, is one-half of a washed-up '60s pop-music act, Sonny and Cher. Sonny is Sonny Bono, 34, songwriter and producer, Cher's husband and string-puller. Four years after conquering pop with "I Got You, Babe," they are off the charts, deeply in debt to the I.R.S. and playing nightclubs as an oldies act. But it was here that they crafted a breezy, tongue-in-cheek riff that cast Sonny as the stooge for Cher's hilarious put-downs. When CBS put them on the air (at first as a summer fill-in), they clicked. *The Sonny and Cher Comedy Hour* topped the ratings until the pressure took a toll: they split up, in life as in their act, in the spring of 1974.

FOR THE FIRST time since she married Sonny at only 17, Cher found herself alone—a single, working mom to Chastity, 4. Okay, finding a new man isn't too hard for Cher: soon record mogul David Geffen was sharing her $2 million estate. But finding success on her own wasn't as easy. Cher's solo TV show tanked after one season, in spring 1976. Its time slot was taken that fall by ... Sonny and Cher, back as an act, if not as a couple.

But the new show (and new boyfriend) didn't last. Geffen, like Sonny, was a control freak; Cher craved freedom. She got more than she bargained for with her new flame, Gregg Allman of Allman Brothers Band fame. Nine days after marrying the hard-partying rocker in June 1975, Cher filed for divorce. But why keep it simple? Soon after, she unfiled, gamely helped Allman with drug therapy and, in the summer of 1976, gave birth to Elijah Blue Allman. Yet just as the beat goes on, so did Gregg's partying. Finally, in 1977, Cher gave up

on Gregg. Soon the quiet, reassuring presence in her life was ... Gene Simmons, the Kabuki-painted tongue-twirler of shock-rock band Kiss.

At the decade's end, Cher is off TV and her albums are tanking. So she's cuddling with Gene, bathing Elijah, taking up est—and talking retirement. "I want to do other things besides being a performer," she told PEOPLE in 1979. Cher—we *Believe* you.

FEATHERED FRIEND Sonny holds Chastity at the pinnacle of the couple's TV success in 1973. Cher put together the duo's duds in the '60s, while Bob Mackie designed most of her memorable '70s outfits.

MASKED MAN Cher huddles with Gene Simmons in 1979—he's hiding because at the time Kiss only appeared in make-up. Despite his image, "He's sweet and warm," Cher said.

PARTY'S OVER Cher split with Gregg Allman nine days after the wedding, then came back to help him fight drugs. Finally, she told PEOPLE, "I just didn't have the juice anymore."

DARK LADY Cher wowed fans at a 1978 Long Island gig. Her songs often played off her French/Armenian/Cherokee heritage, from "Half-Breed" to "Gypsies, Tramps and Thieves."

STALKED Jackie was plagued by paparazzi, most notably by Ron Galella, who took this 1971 shot. A court order finally prohibited him from coming within 30 feet of Jackie and her children.

Jackie O

A widow once more, the former First Lady got a job—and a life

TOURISTS In the early '70s, Jackie took John Jr. and Caroline to the Greek isle of Skorpios, where she and Onassis had staged their surprise 1968 wedding.

ONCE THE WHOLLY OWNED subsidiary of two of the world's most powerful men, Jackie Onassis spent much of the 1970s declaring her personal independence, even as she presided over the teenage years of Caroline and John Jr. After Aristotle Onassis died in Paris in March 1975 (Jackie was in New York at the time), she received $26 million from his estate, the lion's share of which went to Christina Onassis, Jackie's stepdaughter/nemesis.

Like millions of women in the '70s, 46-year-old Jackie set out to find a job. In the fall of 1975 she began toiling as a consulting editor at Viking Press at $200 a week (even as she was putting the finishing touches on her weekend retreat in New Jersey's fox-hunting region). She assumed an active role in New York social life and began speaking out to save such landmarks as Grand Central Terminal. But as for the big question—how's her love life?—most of her escorts, including well-known newspaper writer Pete Hamill, appeared to be no more than convenient squires.

ELTON JOHN

Pop's high-flying Rocket Man finally came down to earth

SPARKLE PLENTY Elton glittered on a 1975 tour: His wild styles helped distance him from his father, a stiff-upper-lip squadron leader in Britain's Royal Air Force.

CAPTAIN FANTASTIC'S joy ride through the '70s was all about closets: first he entertained us with the dazzling duds he pulled out of them—then he moved us by coming out of them altogether, becoming one of the first major stars to declare openly his bisexuality. More than a great showman, he earned fans' respect as a gifted talent, thrilling audiences with his energetic concerts, conquering radio and the pop charts with the series of hits he wrote with lyricist Bernie Taupin—*Bennie and the Jets, Crocodile Rock, Rocket Man*—and winning acclaim from the critics for the strength of his albums.

Elton over-played the pop star role in the early '70s: He owned a flotilla of cars worth $750,000, a $50,000 passel of eyeglasses, a 37-acre estate and—oh, yeah— an entire British soccer team.

But as he turned 30 in 1978, the pudgy, balding Brit (born Reginald Dwight) who had turned himself into campy superstar Elton John, was ready to reinvent himself again. After six years of nonstop

KEY-BORED? Not with Elton at the controls. He began playing when he was four: As in this 1973 show, he often used the piano as a springboard for handstands, cartwheels and other shenanigans.

TALL TALE Elton's outsized persona made him the perfect choice to play the Pinball Wizard in director Ken Russell's outrageously overboard 1975 movie of The Who's classic rock opera, *Tommy*.

touring and recording, "There was no burning spark left," he told PEOPLE. "To sing *Rocket Man* again was just digging up the dregs." He had revealed his bisexuality in 1976; now he underwent a hair transplant, sold off his pyramid of peepers, even said he'd retire. But a star like Elton John needs applause. Like the bitch in his song, he'd be back.

mary tyler moore

A comic genius and role model, she was every gal's best pal

OUR GANG Moore's TV family: from left, Gavin MacLeod, Valerie Harper, Ed Asner, Mary, Ted Knight, Cloris Leachman. Harper and Leachman starred in spin-offs.

FOR SIX GLORIOUS years, Mary Tyler Moore and her sitcom troupe captured the pulse of the searching '70s, exploring a brave new world where single women pursued careers, built "families" of friends and co-workers, even (gasp!) had sex lives. Raised in Los Angeles from age 9, Mary trained as a dancer and debuted on TV as appliance-peddling pixie "Happy Hotpoint." It took her six years to land a major role, as Laura Petrie on the classic *Dick Van Dyke* show, where she first displayed her wit and sparkle. Mary's early marriage to Richard Meeker didn't last, despite the birth of son Richie, and in 1963 she married TV producer Grant Tinker. Hard times followed: she suffered a miscarriage and dis-covered she was diabetic, while her career was put on hold. But a 1969 special with Van Dyke led to the offer of a CBS series. And when Mary Richards—single, sensible yet vulnerable—threw her hat in the air and flashed that incandescent smile, a generation of women discovered they'd found a new best friend.

CLINT EASTWOOD

A shooting star made the moviegoer's day

HE EARNED cult acclaim as the cheroot-chomping, serape-swaddled "Man with No Name" in a trio of '60s spaghetti westerns directed by Sergio Leone. By 1972, movie audiences everywhere knew Clint Eastwood's name: he was the world's top box-office draw. And no wonder: the chiseled good looks and no-nonsense air left his male fans envious—and their girlfriends swooning.

In 1971 the cowboy star took a gamble, starring as Harry Callahan in *Dirty Harry*, a revenge fantasy in which a modern-day cop played judge, jury and executioner to a serial murderer. The film became a huge hit and spawned four follow-ups. But Eastwood, long one of Hollywood's few paragons of domestic tranquility, shocked his fans in 1979 when he ditched Maggie, his wife since 1953, who had supported him in his lean years by working as a model. Clint's trophy gal: blond temptress Sondra Locke, his co-star in 1977's *The Gauntlet*. Never married, they split in the late '80s.

CRUISIN' Breaking out of westerns, Clint gave up horses for horsepower in two 1971 films, *Play Misty for Me* and *Dirty Harry*.

IN DENIAL In 1978 Clint and Sondra still claimed to be only "good friends."

Bette Midler

No vamp, no bombshell, she was a camp tramp in a clamshell

LIKE AN APHRODITE on amphetamines, Bette Midler and her alter ego, The Divine Miss M, presided over the mainstream embrace of the campy, trashy style long popular in theatrical and gay circles. In fact, it was in the gay bathhouses of New York City that Honolulu-born Bette first strapped on her platform shoes and brought down the house.

Bette delighted in what she was selling—"sleaze with ease"—and her joy was infectious. Only 29 in 1975, the 5'1" dynamo returned to Broadway, site of her smash one-woman show in 1973, and topped herself with her *Clams on the Half Shell Revue*. Recycling risqué Sophie Tucker jokes, fronting the trashy Harlettes and belting out hits like "Friends" and "Delta Dawn," she proved herself a dynamo of versatility. Next on her to-do list: TV or the the movies. But hold the sitcoms, please. "I couldn't cut that Mary Tyler Moore–Rhoda crap," allowed the ever-gracious divinity.

TRASH WITH FLASH
"I wouldn't say I invented tack," Bette bragged to PEOPLE in 1975, "but I definitely brought it to its present high popularity."

Barry Manilow

To cheers (and jeers), he sang his heart out

HE MAY HAVE WRITTEN the songs the whole world sang in the '70s, but Barry Manilow often got no respect—not from critics who called him wimpy, not even from himself. Despite scoring thirteen hit singles in a four-year period (think "Mandy" and "At the Copa"), despite being the king of ad jingles (Band-Aid, McDonald's, and others), despite being the producer-arranger who helped Bette Midler ascend to stardom— "To himself, Barry's still zero," a friend told PEOPLE. At a time when stars like Liza and Cher often discoed the night away, he was a virtual recluse.

An only child, Manilow was raised in Brooklyn by his mother; his father left the family when Barry was 2. An early marriage failed, and he once told PEOPLE: "I don't want to share my life with anybody." Maybe so, but he still connects with a large, adoring public. Only the lonely know why.

Bruce Springsteen

A working-class hero made "Joisey" noisy—and cool

ART WAS GETTING THE BEST of rock in the early '70s, as pompous British bands like Yes and Pink Floyd toured big arenas with massive stage shows—as later skewered in Rob Reiner's '85 parody movie *This Is Spinal Tap*. But Bruce Springsteen, a.k.a. "The Boss," put an end to that. Busting out of the gritty boardwalks of New Jersey's seashore resorts, Bruce electrified audiences with music that took rock back to its rockabilly roots and with words that found poetry in everyday life—in old cars, screen doors and highway signs. In an age when pop culture was becoming ever more packaged, Springsteen was authentic and unpasteurized. (Yes, he ended up buying a mansion in Beverly Hills and marrying a model, Julianne Phillips— but that was in the '80s—and they later divorced.) In the '70s, Bruce made rock matter again, and he proved it all night long in joyous, sweat-drenched, three-hour shows.

SPRING-STEEN "The Boss" went vertical at this 1978 concert.

Sylvester Stallone

Showing off his "classy chassis," he K-Oed the box office

THERE'S A FIRST time for everything, and in December 1976, when a cocky young actor/writer first garnered his own story in PEOPLE, we provided pronunciation tips: "Stallone rhymes with unknown." Not for long. That article heralded the release of *Rocky,* a movie Stallone had written in three feverish days and nights. James Caan, Burt Reynolds and Ryan O'Neal (Ryan O'Neal?) all bid to play the title role—and though Sly and his wife Sasha were down to $106 in their savings account—he held out to play the part.

Stallone's fee for both writing and starring in the movie was $23,000. Yet within a year, his fairy-tale story of a hard-luck boxer who rides his fists to glory had taken in $54 million (don't worry—he got points). *Rocky*'s success, he said, was a backlash against movies with "no heroes, no human decency." As he liked to point out, Rocky's story mirrored his own climb from the mean streets of Philadelphia to success. And Sly would keep on climbing: In 1979 he traded in Sasha to date fellow movie jock Susan Anton

FLAGGING? After *Rocky*'s triumph, Sly stumbled with 1978's *F.I.S.T* and *Paradise Alley.*

LIZA MINNELLI

Singer, dancer, partyer and lover, she had pizzazz—with four z's

IF LIFE ISN'T A CABARET, somebody forgot to tell Liza. The supercharged star scrawled her signature across the excessive '70s—but then, she had a head start. As the daughter of Judy Garland and director Vincente Minnelli, she grew up with her godfather Ira Gershwin hanging around the piano and later sang duets with Frank Sinatra. At age 19, she won Broadway's Tony Award; at 26, she won an Oscar for *Cabaret*.

Turning 30 in 1976, Liza was divorced from her first husband, songwriter/singer Peter Allen—who found fame after they split—and had been happily married since 1974 to Jack Haley Jr. (yes, the son of the Tin Man in *The Wizard of Oz*). She was getting set to star in Martin Scorsese's *New York, New York*. But when the Studio 54 era hit, Liza's passion for partying took over. Her personal life—and then her career—whirled into a spiral of self-destruction. The good news: In 1999 she returned to Broadway in a hit one-woman show.

WILKOMMEN
Sexy, funny Liza exerted a larger-than-life attraction: between husbands, her boyfriends included Desi Arnaz Jr., an aristocrat from Paris and a playboy from Brazil.

WANTED: MAN OF STEEL may have been one of the toughest casting calls in Hollywood history. When Warner Bros. set out to bring America's beloved Superman to the screen, it needed a magical mix in the leading character: great body, winsome charm—not to mention the ability to look convincing in that silly suit. As PEOPLE recapped the search, Steve McQueen was too fat, Sly Stallone too Italian, Robert Redford too expensive and Clint Eastwood too busy. So Warner gambled on a preppy young unknown, Christopher Reeve.

The 25-year-old was the anti-Stallone: the son of a Yale prof, he graduated from Cornell, then enrolled at New York City's famous Juilliard School, where he befriended Robin Williams. He starred as bigamist Ben Harper on daytime soap *Love of Life*, then played opposite Kate Hepburn on Broadway in 1976's *A Matter of Gravity.*

In 1995 Reeve would be paralyzed in a horse-riding accident, an ordeal he met with the same humility and optimism that characterized his early ascent to stardom. After *Superman,* Reeve kept his Manhattan studio apartment, played piano for 90 minutes a day and drove a battered 1970 Pinto. Isn't that what Clark Kent would have done?

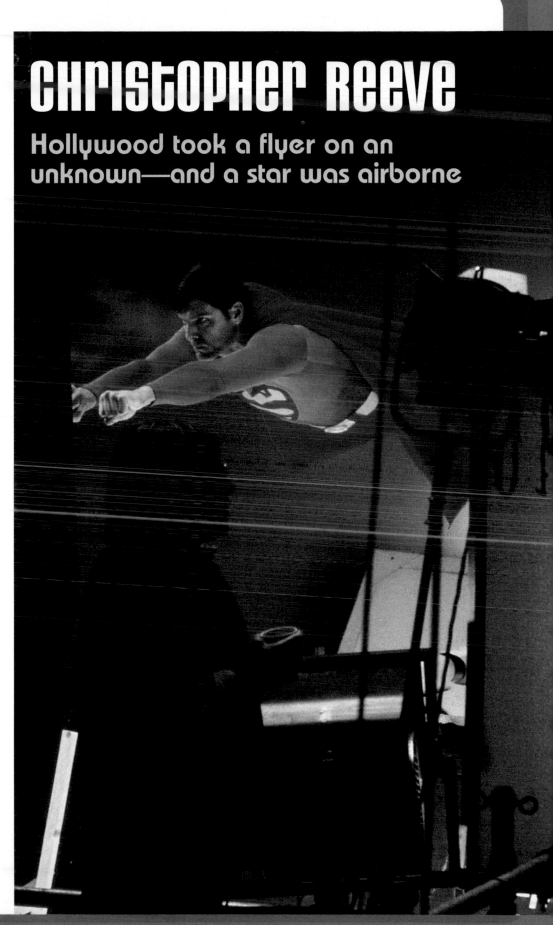

CHRISTOPHER REEVE
Hollywood took a flyer on an unknown—and a star was airborne

IN HARNESS Reeve on the set with a techie; he insisted on doing all his own stunt work in the film. For one take he hung from a crane 240 ft. above New York City's East River.

ABBA

Absolut Pop: Four Swedish songbirds conquered the charts

A$$A: Sweden's #1 export, they outsold Volvo.

IF A QUARTET OF LIVERPUDLIANS could write the sound track for the '60s, why couldn't four Scandinavians do the same for the '70s? That's just what ABBA did—and if you're a fan, you'll know the quartet's name is an acronym for its pair of loving couples: Singer Agnetha Fältskog and guitarist Björn Ulvaeus married in 1971, while singer Anni-Frid Lyngstad and keyboardist Benny Andersson preferred a "Stockholm marriage" (i.e., unblessed by clergy).

Powered by the catchy, melodic ditties of Björn and Benny, ABBA first captured Europe, winning the 1974 Eurovision song contest with "Waterloo." Soon the rest of the world was bopping to "Dancing Queen" and "Fernando": one date in a 6,200-seat London hall drew 3.5 million ticket requests. Björn to be wild? Not this crew. Off the road, they retreated to estates on Stockholm's suburban island of Lidingö with their kids. But fame took its toll: the group split up, and both couples were kaput by 1981.

peter Frampton

Hair today, gone tomorrow: power pop's poster boy had a rapid rise—and a fast fall

PETER WHO? Talk about an overnight sensation: Though he'd paid his dues on the British rock scene as a member of The Herd and Humble Pie, singer/guitarist Peter Frampton was unknown to most American listeners until the release of his live double album in 1976. Capturing Frampton's soaring, melodic lead guitar and his innovative use of the catchy, echoing Vocoder device ("Do you feel like I do-woo-woo"), *Frampton Comes Alive* became the fastest-selling album in the the music business to date. For female fans, Frampton's appeal was pitched somewhere south of the eardrums: his long cascade of golden locks and his clean-cut features had earned him the nickname "The Face" in Britain—and now they earned his poster a place on millions of teen bedroom walls. But there was to be no second act for Frampton: His follow-up albums didn't come alive, he was stuck in the movie stinker *Sgt. Pepper* and, by the end of the decade, rock's golden boy was eating, well, humble pie.

MANE MAN
Frampton saluted New York City fans in 1977. His elfin size (5'7", 115 lbs.) packed major charm. After an amicable 1976 divorce from Brit Mary Lovett, he dated Milwaukee-born Penny McCall.

DIANA ROSS

Motown's '60s queen reigned Supreme as a solo diva in the '70s

SECOND ACTS can be tough in American life, but Diana Ross morphed effortlessly from being one-third of Motown's singing Supremes in '69 to becoming one of the three top female movie stars in the world in '79 (with Barbra Streisand and Faye Dunaway). But behind the scenes of Ross's glittering ride—an Oscar nomination for '72's *Lady Sings the Blues*, more movie success in '75's *Mahogany*, a run of hit songs—lurked plenty of heartbreak.

In 1977 she divorced Robert Silberstein, her husband of six years and father of her three daughters. Then she battled perhaps an even more important man in her life—Motown czar Barry Gordy, who had taken a 16-year-old nobody and made her a Supreme being. When Gordy declared her too old (at 34) to play Dorothy in 1978's *The Wiz*, she fought him tooth and nail, won the part and eased on down, eased on down the road. Two decades later, she's still easin'—and pleasin'.

THEY BLASTED into the '70s out of Gary, Ind., as the chino-wearing kings of bubble-gum pop, headed by an adorable 10-year-old frontman. And they blasted into the '80s as the Afro-topped, gold-lamé-clad kings of funk-driven disco, headed by a sensational 20-year-old frontman. The man in front, of course, was Michael Jackson (in truth, the brothers' act was always Michael-plus-four). But the Jacksons' world was spinning almost as fast as their leader; by the end of the decade, the kid with the electrifying dance moves was starting to carve out an independent career.

In 1975 the Jacksons left their longtime label, Motown, and joined Epic, where Michael cut his own deal as a solo act. In 1978 he ventured into film, starring as a rubber-legged Scarecrow in *The Wiz*, with his old Motown friend Diana Ross. Yet that year PEOPLE found Michael still living at home in Encino, Calif., with parents Katherine and Joe, and sisters LaToya, 22, and Janet, 12. "I'd like to branch out into things that will give me longevity, perhaps choreography or writing songs for other people," he said.

The next year, Michael began to make good on his pledge. He released the solo album *Off the Wall*—and that's how it went over, generating a slew of hits, including the infectious "Don't Stop 'til You Get Enough." As the '80s began, their chief Thriller was waiting in the wings.

FAMILY Jermaine split in 1975; brother Randy joined. Michael's in the middle, and then you have ... uhh ... the other brothers

NOT IN KANSAS *The Wiz* was the most expensive musical ever filmed as of its release in 1978. The fab four: Nipsey Russell (Tinman), Michael Jackson (Scarecrow), Diana Ross (Dorothy), Ted Ross (Cowardly Lion).

THE JACKSON FIVE

E pluribus unum: From many, one

KING TUT

Mummy-mania ruled when Tut kicked butt

"FUNKY TUT" Steve Martin walked like an Egyptian in his stand-up act.

THE MOST UNLIKELY SENSATION of the '70s? Well, how about a teenage pharaoh who died around 1350 B.C.? When Egypt sent its "Treasures of Tutankhamen" exhibit to America, the show became the hottest ticket in the land. As Tut-mania swept the country, eager crowds in Washington pitched tents and slept al fresco to hold their place in line, while New Orleans officials sent helicopters aloft to supervise a gridlocked pharaoh's flock.

"I see wonderful things," archaeologist Howard Carter had declared upon opening Tut's sealed tomb in 1922. Five decades later, U.S. marketers produced a host of wonderful (sort of) things: You could wear Tut jewelry, sit on a Tut chair, sleep in Tut sheets—the proliferation of paraphernalia produced a full-blown Tut-glut. Tut even achieved the pinnacle of '70s fame: He was parodied on *Saturday Night Live* in Steve Martin's hilarious "King Tut" number, complete with a saxophonist in shades emerging from a sarcophagus. Tut uncommon!

MIKHAIL BARYSHNIKOV

It's a bird! It's a plane! No, it's the one man we liked to see in tights

AS THE PRINCE OF Russia's famed Kirov Ballet, Mikhail Baryshnikov had it all: an adoring public, a country dacha—even a housekeeper. But he longed for freedom, and in 1974 he made a daring leap to liberty, defecting while on tour in Toronto. Within four years, "Misha" had not only emerged as the world's finest classical dancer but also vaulted out of the esoteric world of ballet into pop-idol status: The Travolta of high culture captivated nonballet audiences and won an Oscar nomination in 1977's *The Turning Point.*

Defying the stereotype of the effeminate male dancer, Misha was a heartbreaker, sashaying with Liza Minnelli in New York City discos and pas de deuxing offstage with partner Gelsey Kirkland as well as less famed dancers (he was one superstar who was never rotten to the corps). Actress Jessica Lange hooked up with—but never married—the leaping Latvian in 1976; their daughter Alexandra was born in 1981. They later split up, but Misha, 52 in 2000, is still hoofing his heart out.

SOAR SPOT Misha achieves lift-off in 1975. His athleticism thrilled ballet lovers, while his blue eyes stirred hearts. "I adore women," he confided to PEOPLE in 1978.

George Lucas

Beholding a void, he created the droid

A LONG TIME FROM NOW, in a galaxy far, far away, the *Star Wars* phenomenon may seem more like a religion than a movie. It may seem that Han Solo, Darth Vader, Luke Skywalker and all the rest were not so much created as revealed, like sci-fi scripture. Yet created they were, and by a young director who was only 33 when he released the 1977 sci-fi landmark that swallowed *Jaws* on its way to becoming Hollywood's most lucrative movie to date. George Lucas, who wrote, directed and produced the monster hit, later claimed that he'd worked 361 16-hour days in the year before its release.

When PEOPLE caught up with the reclusive director in 1978, he was unspoiled by success, driving a '67 Camaro and living in a modest house in a San Francisco suburb with wife Marcia, one of the editors who

cut *Star Wars*. Lucas would later buy a sprawling, 3,000-acre spread he christened the Skywalker Ranch; by 1984 a divorce from Marcia would be pending, and Linda Ronstadt was residing on the ranch.

In his 1973 hit *American Graffiti,* Lucas had fondly portrayed his own adolescent cruising days in Modesto, Calif. He credited his recovery from a near-fatal auto crash two days before his graduation from high school with engendering the humanitarian, nonsectarian faith expressed in the *Stars Wars* concept of "The Force." As the life-long devotee of comic books told PEOPLE, "My main reason for making *Star Wars* was to give young people an honest, wholesome fantasy life the way we had. All they've got now is *Kojak* and *Dirty Harry.*" Mission accomplished, Mr. Lucas.

DOWN TIME Lucas and a grumpy Alec Guinness (Obi-Wan Kenobi) waited to shoot in Tunisia, where the scenes of desert planet Tatooine were filmed. Guinness came to dislike the movie's obsessive fans.

Steven Spielberg

He made movie history at 27 when Jaws first opened wide

THE BIGGEST MOVIE STAR of 1975 was a plastic shark named "Bruce." Not long after he surfaced on theater screens in *Jaws,* his movie had become Hollywood's biggest grosser to date. *Jaws* cut quite a wake: it created a genre, the summer blockbuster, that is still going strong. But "Bruce" wasn't the real star of *Jaws,* nor was its fine cast—Richard Dreyfuss, Roy Scheider and Robert Shaw. No, the breakout star of this show was its director, Steven Spielberg, who was only 27 when it was released.

Bitten early by the movie bug, Spielberg made his first film when he was in grade school, won his first award when he was 13, and was directing Joan Crawford for television at age 23.

Three years after *Jaws* (only his second major film), Spielberg would create a sci-fi classic, *Close Encounters of the Third Kind.* Meanwhile, the workaholic filmmaker would enjoy a close encounter of his own: In 1978 actress Amy Irving moved into "the house that *Jaws* built." Married in 1985, they split up in 1989. Spielberg's wife since 1991 has been actress Kate Capshaw.

CLOSE ENCOUNTERS Richard Dreyfuss starred in Spielberg's two '70s hits.

ME AND MY BIG MOUTH Spielberg mugged with a friend on Martha's Vineyard during the location shooting for *Jaws.*

CHARLiE'S ANGELS

Don't adjust your TV —that jiggle was intentional

IT WAS A FORMULA made in Hollywood heaven: take three gorgeous young gals, cast them as undercover detectives, give them snazzy hairdos and wardrobes to die for (except for bras), then set them running across a TV screen. The result was the cheesy, chesty *Charlie's Angels,* which became an overnight smash when it hit the tube in September 1976. First among

equals was Farrah Fawcett-Majors (Jill), whose haircut inspired a zillion new dos—and whose anatomically correct poster inspired a zillion male fantasies. Married to "bionic man" Lee Majors (they split in '79), Farrah bolted the show after the first season, returning only in occasional guest shots.

Beauteous-but-blah Jaclyn Smith (Kelly) stayed with the show for its

entire five-year run. But Kate Jackson (Sabrina) bridled at its endless titillations, balking at a scene requiring a braless run in a foot race and publicly dissing the show as fluff. Her rebellion peaked after she married actor Andrew Stevens in 1979, and she was fired. But in Hollywood, as in heaven, *Angels* never die: a big-screen version is coming soon to a theater near you.

HALO DOLLIES Sure, you know Farrah, Kate and Jaclyn. But can you name the latter-day Angels? If you said Cheryl Ladd as Kris, Shelley Hack as Tiffany and Tanya Roberts as Julie—take a bow!

This sexy crew brought us the triple entendre

WHEN THE FREE-WHEELING sexual frankness of the '70s hit the TV screen, it was often packaged as a naughty sideshow of innuendo and revealing outfits. But with the right cast, the concept clicked. Case in point: *Three's Company*, a knock-off of the British hit *Man About the House,* which debuted on ABC in 1977. In a day when the concept of separate sexes sharing an apartment without sharing vows (or beds) seemed daring, the show's premise had single straight guy John Ritter rooming with two "just-buddies"— bodacious bimbo Suzanne Somers and perky Joyce DeWitt. The show became a hit in its first year, driven by Somers' classic ditzy blond and Ritter's boyish charm. Though the show ran until 1984, its first three years were its best. In 1980 Somers, by then a superstar, demanded a huge pay hike: instead, her role was reduced and she literally "called in" her part on the phone each week. Today Somers is on infomercials hawking fitness gear and Ritter is thriving: in one recent role, he squired '90s TV icon Ally McBeal.

THREE'S COMPANY

ROOMIES WITH A VIEW Many bashed the show for its non-stop sexy chatter— and it didn't help that it shared a network hour with a show dedicated to breaking all of TV's rules, *Soap.*

POSTER GIRL This Farrah pose was an icon of a racy era.

THE OLYMPIANS

Going for the gold, they stole our hearts

NADIA COMANECI

THE AIRBORNE ROMANIAN was only 14 when she scored the first-ever flawless marks in Olympic gymnastics at the 1976 Games in Montreal—not just once, but seven times. Tiny (5 ft., 86 lbs.) and highly focused, Nadia excelled thanks to her calmness and hyper-flexibility. Under Svengali of the balance beam Bela Karolyi, the ponytailed prodigy was intense—some said dour—but she loosened up over time, moving to America and marrying red-white-and-blue gymnast Bart Connor in 1996.

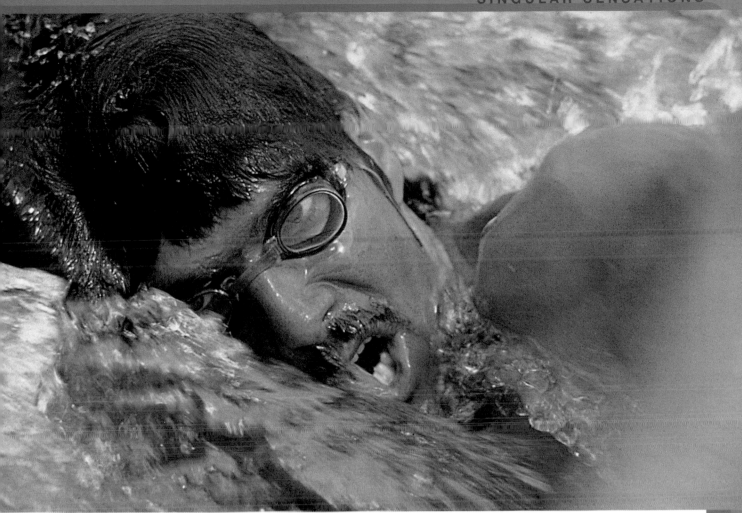

MARK SPITZ

THE SPLASHY SPITZ WAS one of the first Olympians to find crossover success as a pop-culture superstar. After he Speedoed to an unprecedented seven gold medals in the 1972 Munich Games, his handsome mug graced millions of posters, while he raked in millions in endorsements. Today Spitz prospers as a motivational speaker and real estate agent.

BRUCE JENNER

THE 1976 DECATHLON champion shared credit for his success with wife Chrystie, a onetime stewardess. Post-Olympics, Bruce became the face of Wheaties, and even the Jenners' dog Bertha fetched a deal with General Mills. Bruce and Chrystie eventually parted ways; today Jenner and wife Kris preside over a decathlon's worth of kids—ten—from his three marriages. Call him a cereal dad.

In numbers too big to ignore,
women banded together to say:
No one's gonna keep us down!

I AM WOMAN

HELEN REDDY

Her anthem gave feminists their marching orders

"I HATE THE SONG, but my wife makes me play it" was many a deejay's lament, for Helen Reddy's "I Am Woman" became an instant women's classic after its '72 release. Accepting a Grammy for the song, Reddy thanked "God, because She makes everything possible." The Australian-born singer came to New York in 1966 when she was 24, with 3-year-old daughter Traci, and married agent Jeff Wald, her tough-talking manager; son Jordan arrived in 1973. "I Am Woman" sparked a string of follow-up hits, a TV

variety show and movie roles, but by the end of the decade the saucy Aussie's career was fading.

A reluctant icon, Reddy once told PEOPLE, "I'm a feminist, but it's not what I do for a living. I have a career and marriage happening all at the same time, and that's the example I set." She and Wald divorced in the early '80s, and she wed drummer Milton Ruth in 1983 (they amicably split in 1996). Reddy claims she has no plans to marry again, asking, "What can any man give me that I can't give myself?"

LIGHTNING ROD
After "I Am Woman," shock rocker Alice Cooper called Reddy "the Queen of House-wife Rock." She stood by the song, even though she was not as militant as its defiant lyrics implied.

ERICA JONG

A prolific pioneer unbuttoned her heroine's fantasies

"**A FEMALE** version of *Tropic of Cancer,*" was fellow writer Henry Miller's take on Erica Jong's *Fear of Flying,* a paean to sex for the sake of sex, albeit from a woman's angle. Critics, male and female, thought her racy 1973 novel, a thinly disguised autobiography, was more about revolving bedmates than raising consciousness. But Jong's notion of "zipless" fun resonated with '70s women seeking sexual freedom. Her heroine, Isadora Wing, kept evolving, having a baby in *How to Save Your Own Life* (1977) and becoming a single mom in *Parachutes & Kisses* (1984).

A self-described "left-leaning Jewish feminist and devout pagan," Jong was born Erica Mann in New York City in 1942. Divorced three times, Jong has one daughter, Molly, and is now married (aptly) to divorce lawyer Ken Burroughs. In a mid-life memoir, *Fear of Fifty,* she describes the plight of the women of her times, terming them the "Whiplash Generation": they were raised to be Doris Day but wanted to be Gloria Steinem. Though she's written six volumes of poetry, nine novels and five nonfiction books, Jong admits, "The zipless thing will be on my tombstone."

GLORIA STEINEM

She brought power and glory to the sisterhood

ARTICULATE, ATTRACTIVE and energetic, Gloria Steinem was the most famous face of the women's movement in the '70s. From fighting for reproductive freedom to advocating fair treatment in the workplace, Steinem paved the way. She helped create such milestones as *Ms.* magazine, the Women's Action Alliance and the National Women's Political Caucus, collaborating with such like-minded feminist pioneers as Bella Abzug.

Born in Toledo, Ohio, in 1934, Steinem graduated from Smith College in 1956, then spent two years in India before settling down to a successful, high profile career as a freelance reporter in New York. One of her eye-opening articles was a firsthand exposé of the Playboy empire, for which Steinem posed as a Bunny, donning ears and tail. After many well-publicized romances, the breast cancer survivor remains unmarried, living alone with her cat. "Marriage is something I would consider only out of severe depression," the witty activist told PEOPLE in 1974.

Steinem is still manning —womanning?—the front lines of feminism. She once said, "I thought I would do this for two or three years and then go home to my real life." Thirty years later, this *is* her life.

GENDER GAP
"A woman needs a man like a fish needs a bicycle," Gloria Steinem once quipped.

49

STAR SEARCH

THE RIGHTS STUFF Hollywood's hoi polloi gathered to tout the ERA. Even we can't name 'em all, but here goes (from the left, bottom row): Harvey Korman, Peter Yarrow, Dory Previn, Shirley MacLaine, Bella Abzug, Susan Blakely, Jane Fonda, Kate Jackson, Adrienne Barbeau, Maxine Waters. Middle: Esther Rolle, David Frost, Mary Kay Place, unidentified, Jody Baker, Cicely Tyson, Marlo Thomas, Joanna Shimkus Poitier, Polly Bergen, Jessica Walter, Lily Tomlin, unidentified, Donna Mills, Deborah Raffin,

Henry Winkler, Charles Grodin. Back row: Norman Lear,
Billy Davis, Marilyn McCoo, Richard Mulligan, Renee Taylor,
Joseph Bologna, Sydney Poitier, unidentified, Wayne Rogers,
Elliot Gould, Chevy Chase, Joan Hackett, unidentified.

Hollywood celebs came together for equal rights

A WHO'S WHO of Tinseltown liberals opened their wallets when feminism came calling. In 1978, New York Congresswoman Bella Abzug, head of the National Women's Political Caucus, gathered the faithful in a show of support for the embattled Equal Rights Amendment. In striking polka dots and one of her trademark broad-brimmed hats, she posed with the believers, all smiles. But their crusade proved to be in vain. The proposed amendment, which read, in part, "Equality of Rights under the law shall not be denied or abridged by the United States or any state on account of sex," passed Congress in 1972, but was not ratified by the necessary 38 states before the July 1982 deadline. Passage of the ERA remains a central concern for many women's groups.

Responding to critics of the measure—and addressing many of the misconceptions circulated about it—Gloria Steinem wrote, "The ERA has nothing to do with whether gays adopt children, does not increase the power of the federal government, does not lead to unisex toilets nor is it 'pro-abortion.' " Despite the ERA's defeat, its supporters had paved the way for an era when Hollywood stars would publicly embrace a host of political causes.

GOD BLESS AMERICA—where we address the most urgent social issues of the age in absurd made-for-TV spectacles. And they don't get any more spectacular—or absurd—than this one: With the feminist movement at its controversial height, 60 million people tuned in to the tennis tussle between the "pigs" and the "libs" in September 1973. Billie Jean King, a top women's player in the world at age 29, demolished male chauvinist and former Wimbledon champ Bobby Riggs in straight sets at Houston's Astrodome. Riggs, at 55, had bragged that no woman could beat a man, no matter how past his prime. He arrived on the court wearing a crown, while King entered borne aloft by a team of half-clad men.

Born Billie Jean Moffitt in 1943, King recalled seeing her first ball game as a child: "What struck me like a thunderbolt was that there were no women on that baseball diamond." She abandoned softball for tennis and went on to win six Wimbledon singles titles. In 1971 she became the first female athlete to win more than $100,000 in prize money in a single season.

BATTLE OF THE SEXES

The racquet queen sent the piggish pretender packing in straight sets

NO LOVE MATCH In a circus-like atmosphere, complete with silly costumes, Billie Jean proved that Bobby's boasts were as empty as his bodice. The $100,000 purse was the largest paid for a single match to date. As the brilliant '70s ad slogan proclaimed: "You've come a long way, baby."

A forceful pioneer, King revolutionized women's tennis by demanding equal pay, founding a players' union for women and launching the first women-only pro circuit. Her long struggle benefited women athletes across all playing fields, as women's college sports scholarships increased.

Billie Jean married fellow college student Larry King in 1965, and he became her manager. But in 1981, the year she retired as an active player, she was outed as a bisexual in a palimony suit; she and Larry divorced in 1988. An enduring hero to many, she is now a TV commentator.

American Pie

We cherished down-home hoe-downs and long-lost hometowns

John Denver
He winged us aloft on a natural high

Maybe it was our desire to return to a simpler, purer time. Maybe we were tired of a decade of America-bashing. Whatever the reason, with his Dutch-boy haircut, his granny glasses and his voice as clear as the mountain air he invoked in his songs, John Denver struck a chord. Denver—born Henry John Deutschendorf in Roswell, N.Mex.—expressed a deep '70s yearning to escape a complex age. To the scorn of sophisticates, his songs paid homage to nature, love, family and "country" values. What would you expect from a man who spent his boyhood summers on a farm in Corn, Okla.?

Sixties coffee-house folk music was already on the wane as

John Denver left Texas Tech in 1964 and joined the Chad Mitchell Trio, later known as Denver, Boise and Johnson. When the going-nowhere group disbanded in 1969, it was Denver who nobly assumed their $40,000 debt.

Money worries would soon be history, as Denver—an Air Force brat raised in towns throughout the Southwest—became one of the most successful recording artists and live performers in the world. "Take Me Home, Country Roads" was a million-seller in 1971. "Rocky Mountain High," inspired by Denver and wife Annie's move to Aspen, Colo., went platinum the following year. And you couldn't turn on a radio in 1974 without hearing "Annie's Song," "Sunshine on My Shoulders" or "Back Home Again"—each of them a mega-hit. Appropriately, Colorado's then-governor John Vanderhoof named John the state's poet laureate.

The words and melodies that some viewed as saccharine and naive, and others as sweetly honest, continued, with 1975's "Thank God I'm a Country Boy" and "I'm Sorry." It seemed Denver could do no wrong. Even his screen debut, a folksy turn opposite comedian George Burns in the 1977 film *Oh, God!*, earned accolades.

Denver's appealing, boy-next-door image was largely accurate. Nevertheless, his marriage to Annie endured well-publicized ups and downs: she finally asked for a divorce on their 15th anniversary, in 1982. He married singer Cassandra Delaney in 1988, but they divorced shortly after the birth of daughter Jesse Belle in 1989. What John later called a dark night of the soul followed: he was arrested in Aspen in the summer of 1993 for drunken driving; a year later he totaled a Porsche. Both raised eyebrows among those for whom he had been an icon of wholesomeness. As he confessed in 1995, "I've had a few difficult years."

But Denver—a hope-springs-eternal optimist who committed a great deal of time and money to the environmental causes he loved—bounced back. In the end, it was his zest for flying, a longtime hobby, that took his life. He was killed on Oct. 12, 1997, when the small experimental aircraft that he was solo-piloting plunged into California's Monterey Bay. It was an ironic coda to the life of an artist whose songs lifted so many hearts, and whose first major success as a songwriter—a big hit for folkies Peter, Paul and Mary in 1969—was "Leaving on a Jet Plane."

Dolly Parton Golly dang! We dug Dolly's twang

YOU HAD TO LOOK PAST the cascading wigs and the cartoon-like figure—and get to the songs. Once you did, you understood how Dolly Parton could put together a string of more than 20 country hits—many of which she composed herself. Born poor, she was the fourth of 12 children, and her farmer father paid the doctor in cornmeal after her delivery. It was cornmeal well spent.

Arriving in Nashville in 1964, Parton hooked up with TV host Porter Waggoner in '67, and in 1971 had a smash with "Coat of Many Colors." When Emmylou Harris and Maria Muldaur covered Parton songs like "My Tennessee Mountain Home," they helped country music break out of Nashville and enter the mainstream—and Dolly crossed over on her own with "Here You Come Again," which went gold in 1978. By now a major celebrity, she opened her own theme park, Dollywood, then set about conquering Hollywood. Sure enough, she earned an Oscar nomination for her first film role, in 1980's *9 to 5,* and in her spare time wrote its theme song, a No.1 hit on both the pop and country charts. Two decades later, she's still on top—a star for all reasons.

BUSTED Parton does her Daisy Mae act. Her bombshell image often overshadowed her work as a disciplined, intelligent songwriter.

The Waltons
A mountain clan scaled TV's heights

CRITICS LOVED IT, but people weren't tuning in. So CBS launched a flurry of full-page newspaper ads that read, "This Program Is So Beautiful It Has to Die." The gimmick worked: *The Waltons* avoided death-through-cancellation. In fact, the Depression-era drama depicting a homespun, lesson-filled, rose-colored past our grandfathers probably never really enjoyed went on to run for almost a decade.

It all started with *The Homecoming,* a TV-special adaptation of Virginia author Earl Hamner, Jr.'s reminiscences of an Appalachian boyhood. Hamner himself was *The Waltons'* omniscient narrator, observing life through the sympathetic eyes of John-Boy Walton, Hamner's alter ego, played by the appealing Richard Thomas. The show's breakout star, he was (and is) a charmer who still enjoys success on our TV screens.

Each week on Walton's Mountain, patient, understanding John Walton (Ralph Waite), his long-suffering wife Olivia (Michael Learned), and Grandpa and Grandma Walton (veteran actors Will Geer and Ellen Corby) guided their family through crises that depicted both the realities of hardscrabble 1930s existence and the realities of network television—for the Waltons' woes were often wrapped up in neat homilies in one hour flat.

CLOSE-KNIT The show's key stars were the older folks (left to right from top): Learned, Thomas, Waite, Corby and Geer. If you can name the kids—call Regis.

WE ARE FAMILY The Ingalls brood (though they never brooded): from left, Melissa Gilbert, Landon, Grassle, Melissa Sue Anderson.

Little House On the Prairie

It was as corny as Kansas in August—as buttered in L.A.

MICHAEL LANDON seemed to skip a few decades, right there on our TV set. Growing up under "Pa" (Lorne Greene) as *Bonanza*'s Little Joe, his adolescence was protracted over the show's 14-year run. The next thing we knew, Michael had become a "Pa" himself—on another landmark series, *Little House on the Prairie.* So ... What happened to the guy's 20s and 30s?

The real Landon turned his growing-up years to good use. During his career on *Bonanza,* he evolved from actor to writer to director. After that long-running hit left the air, Landon's next move was clear: He became executive producer of his new series. Smart move. For the next nine years, *Little House on the Prairie* enriched our lives—and his pocketbook.

In the series, Landon and Karen Grassle played Charles and Caroline Ingalls, the loving parents of Mary, Laura and Carrie. Based on the fine autobiographical books by pioneer daughter Laura Ingalls Wilder, the program was an affectionate portrayal of 19th century homesteading on the Great Plains. True, *Little House* was largely soap-opera-meets-horse-opera— PEOPLE went so far as to call it "a sort of Sweet 'n Low *Waltons.*" But Landon understood his audience. His show delivered history lessons and basic American values, and will probably always be playing somewhere in syndication. And that's a good thing, for in 1991 Michael Landon— a beloved star and "Pa" to a passel of kids—succumbed to cancer at only 53. Before he left, he carved a place in our memories as wide as his incandescent grin.

Back to the Glory Days
Running on over-drive, we longed for simpler times

Grease OLIVIA NEWTON-JOHN, as the prim Sandy, donned tight black pants and launched into the high-energy dance number "You're the One That I Want" just to prove to Danny Zuko (John Travolta) that she, too, could be cool. The feel-good Broadway show became a great 1978 movie turn for Travolta—his dance in the gym sealed his rep as the era's prime mover.

American Graffiti

AFTER HE WAS OPIE but before he was a Big-Deal Director, Ron Howard (left) starred in George Lucas's 1973 hit about two high-school grads on a final cruise of the hometown strip. The cast included Cindy Williams and Charles Martin Smith (above) as well as Harrison Ford and Richard Dreyfuss.

Happy Days

AAAYYY! Whether playing the hood at Arnold's Drive-In or digging into the milk and cookies at the whitebread Cunninghams', the Fonz ruled. Henry Winkler, one of TV's best pre-Kramer sidekicks, played the '50s biker bad-boy with warmth and sensitivity— and took the show to No. 1 in '76-77.

Crossover Dreams
Country? Rock? Pop? They happily blurred the lines

The Eagles

CRAFTING ROCK and country into a slick blend, the Eagles perfected the laid-back outlaw brand of cool pioneered by the Byrds and others. Their 1975 lineup is above: Randy Meisner, Glenn Frey, Bernie Leadon, Don Felder and drummer Don Henley. (Guitarist Joe Walsh and bassist Timothy B. Schmidt joined up later.) Their songs traced the decade's trajectory, from the sweet daydreams of 1973's "Peaceful, Easy Feeling" to the druggy buzz of 1976's "Hotel California" and "Life in the Fast Lane."

Willie Nelson

WITH HIS GRIZZLED face and nasal twang, this great song-writer, who penned classics like "Crazy" for Pasty Cline and "Hello Walls" for Faron Young in the early '60s, seemed an unlikely candidate for Nashville stardom—at least to country-music execs. So he hooked up with the hippies and rednecks to make Austin, Texas, a new center of country rock. His remake of the 1940s Roy Acuff classic "Blue Eyes Crying in the Rain"—which went gold in 1975—made Willie a superstar. Last time we looked, he was "On the Road Again."

Glen Campbell

HE EARNED HIS SPURS playing guitar for the Beach Boys and Sinatra, then made it on his own in the late '60s, with the soothing "Gentle on My Mind." The '70s brought the Delight, Ark., native his two No. 1 hits: the signature "Rhinestone Cowboy" (1975) and the toe-tapping "Southern Nights" (1977). After a long, ugly fling with drugs (and with two-steppin' teaser Tanya Tucker), he's now good ol' Glen—again.

Johnny Cash

"HELLO, I'm Johnny Cash," the man in black would say, in a voice of quiet intensity—and the audience would go wild. The Arkansas native worked in a Michigan auto factory, then headed to Memphis, where he became pals with Carl Perkins and Jerry Lee Lewis at Sun Records. Overcoming a problem with pills, he scored big hits with "Ring of Fire," "I Walk the Line" and "Folsom Prison Blues." He also scored with June Carter, a member of country music's royal Carter Family; they wed in 1968. When the '70s rolled around, the man with the deep voice (and the deep experience of American life) was in tune with the country craze: he had his own TV show, kept the hits coming, performed at the Nixon White House and was well on his way to a 1992 induction into the Rock and Roll Hall of Fame.

Back to Basics

The '60s hippies forged the trail— now we all embraced Mother Nature

Earth Shoes

THESE ergonomically designed shoes for the health-food crowd actually made the wearer feel shorter—thanks to "negative heel" construction that kept the back of your foot lower than your toes. Sales of the down-at-the-heels clodhoppers soared at first, but they faced an uphill journey: finally, expansion problems and a turn to flashy designs helped sink the faddish footwear.

Denis Hayes

AS THE DECADE BEGAN, the political activism of the '60s spawned two causes that endure: women's liberation and environmentalism. Denis Hayes left a law practice to head up the first Earth Day: April 22, 1970. It is now a major annual event around the world; in 1990 Hayes co-chaired its 20th anniversary.

No Nukes

MUSICIAN DAVID CROSBY told PEOPLE, "You couldn't have bought this list … for the national debt." Joni Mitchell, Jackson Browne, Bruce Springsteen, Bonnie Raitt and other rock heavyweights waived their fees for MUSE—Musicians United for Safe Energy. Apart from raising millions of dollars, the sheer star power of the 1979 tour focused national attention on the issue of safe energy.

Stewart Brand

HIPPIE? TECHIE? Counterculture guru? Stewart Brand, a Stanford-educated Exeter grad, Bay Area Zeitgeist maven, rider of Earth Balls (as in the picture) and onetime Merry Prankster, was all the above. His *Whole Earth Catalogue* was the how-to manual for back-to-the-earth self-reliance, proselytizing about everything from natural vitamins to home cooking in the workplace.

Granola

STORE-BOUGHT was okay—in a crunch. But for *real* crunch, every self-respecting, batik-clad earth mother had her own recipe. The magical mix of oats, seeds, nuts, dried fruits (organic, of course) and honey (unprocessed, natch) was healthful in every way. Then again … one serving had about a million calories.

Back to Nature

HONEY RAISIN
GRANOLA
CEREAL

NET WT. 16 OZS. (1 LB.)

DARK SIDE OF

A dramatic decade filled the headlines with bad trips, tragic ends, national nightmares and spine-tingling events

ELVIS

Fans bid a fond farewell to their King of rock and roll

The Hillbilly Cat from Tupelo, Miss., Elvis Aron Presley got high from performing—he once said, "It's like your whole body gets goose bumps." But after being on top of the show business world for nearly a decade, the King had lost his pop music throne in the mid-'60s: He was an icon from an earlier era, swept aside by the all-conquering Beatles. But against the odds, in a phoenix-like comeback that began in 1968, Elvis proceeded to reclaim his crown. Starting the '70s off with hit records like "The Wonder of You" and "Burning Love," he

BOB WOODWARD & CARL BERNSTEIN

THIS DYNAMIC DUO, known collectively as Woodstein, made an early impression on Robert Redford (Woodward to Dustin Hoffman's Bernstein in the 1976 film *All The President's Men*). Redford learned that the two reporters who broke the story were originally small fish in Washington circles " 'That's a movie,' I said." The two who channeled "Deep Throat" later wrote about Nixon's final days. Woodward (above, right) has moved up the *Post*'s ranks; Bernstein is now a full-time pundit.

JUDGE SIRICA

"MAXIMUM JOHN," a federal judge, handed out tough sentences during the Watergate trials but later went easier on some of the defendants who cooperated with the inquiry. He died in 1992.

MARTHA MITCHELL

A SOUTHERN LADY MACBETH, the Attorney General's outspoken wife, under the influence, threatened to make late-night phone calls to reporters, revealing that her husband had "every Democrat in Washington bugged." The FBI suggested her phone be removed. After Watergate, she forced Mitchell to retire from politics. She died in 1976, at only 57.

JOHN & MO DEAN

TELEGENIC and media-savvy, the Deans survived to live the good life after Watergate. Now an investment banker in Beverly Hills, the former White House counsel John W. Dean III left "the reservation," spent four months in prison and wrote *Blind Ambition*. Wife Maureen wrote her own memoir and two Washington novels.

SAM ERVIN

A TRUE GENTLEMAN, Sen. Ervin, a Democrat from North Carolina, oversaw the Watergate committee in a fair and good-humored manner. He felt sorry for Nixon but also felt compassion for the millions "who lost confidence" in government. He died in 1985, at age 88.

LIVIN' LARGE
"Acting is dull," Brando said, but in *Apocalypse Now,* the portly legend delivered a riveting portrayal of a murderous, renegade colonel.

MARLON BRANDO

The enigmatic star became a contender again

AS THE '70S BEGAN, Marlon Brando was more chump than champ. Long gone were the sexy screen triumphs *A Streetcar Named Desire* and *On the Waterfront.* Brando's stock had fallen so far that his up-front money for 1972's *The Godfather* dropped to $50,000. But appearing in young director Francis Ford Coppola's gangster epic proved to be a wise move. Playing aging Mob boss Don Corleone in a nasal voice that instantly became the stuff of parody, Brando was the dark heart of the hit film hailed by TIME as "an Italian-American *Gone with the Wind.*" Never mind that Brando stayed home from the 1972 Academy Awards ceremony and sent Native American Sacheen Littlefeather to decline his Best Actor Oscar. He continued to make headlines in 1973 with the erotic drama *Last Tango in Paris.* But then it all slipped away again. Noticeably heavier, he teamed with Jack Nicholson for the flop 1976 western *The Missouri Breaks,* when PEOPLE called him "fat, sassy and 51," and appeared in *Superman,* reportedly receiving a $2.8 million fee for a cameo. By now, Brando didn't bother to hide his lack of interest in acting—he worked primarily to bankroll his very private life on a Tahitian atoll.

Brando reunited with Coppola for 1979's sprawling Vietnam drama *Apocalypse Now,* appearing as the film's spooky villain in almost total darkness, allegedly to minimize his reported 300-lb. bulk. Fat jokes have clung to Brando like a cheap suit ever since. Although he received an Oscar nomination for 1989's *A Dry White Season* and delivered a memorable parody of his don role in 1990's *The Freshman,* most of his later work has been forgettable. In the '90s his private life went haywire: in 1990 his son Christian shot and killed his daughter Cheyenne's boyfriend, and Cheyenne committed suicide in 1995.

MOB SCENE After a string of box-office flops, Brando became a hot property once again in 1972, playing the title role in *The Godfather.*

DECADE OF DOWNERS
Face facts: Most '70s news ... was bad news

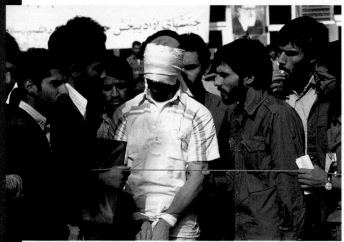

IRAN HOSTAGE CRISIS

YELLOW RIBBONS were tied around old oak trees at the decade's end, anticipating the long-awaited homecoming of the 52 Americans captured at the U.S. Embassy in Tehran, Iran, on Nov. 4, 1979. Their captors, followers of the fierce Islamic militant Ayatollah Ruhollah Khomeini, above, were enraged by America's support of the recently overthrown Shah of Iran. The hostages' demoralizing ordeal worsened when a U.S. rescue attempt ended in failure. Finally, Khomeini and his "government of God" ordered the hostages freed on Jan. 20, 1981, the day Ronald Reagan succeeded Jimmy Carter as President. The Ayatollah died in 1989, and U.S. relations with Iran have slowly improved.

KENT STATE

FEAR AND ANGUISH were etched on the face of teenager Mary Ann Vecchio as she knelt by a body at Kent State University on May 4, 1970, when Ohio National Guardsmen killed four young people and wounded nine during a rally against President Nixon's expansion of the Vietnam War into Cambodia. One guardsman testified that after firing and seeing what had happened, he cried. Subsequent lawsuits brought little comfort: Despite monetary awards as compensation for injuries, no assignment of responsibility for the deaths was ever made. The tragedy boosted the size and vigor of anti-war protests.

THE FALL OF SAIGON

AMERICANS ARE NOT accustomed to losing battles: Our history books resound with victories, from Yorktown to D-Day. So it was a painful sight to see Americans frantically boarding helicopters to flee Saigon, South Vietnam's capital, in April 1975. In that month, after more than 10 years of a massive U.S. military effort in southeast Asia—which had bitterly divided Americans at home—the armies of North Vietnam routed the U.S.-supported forces of South Vietnam. On April 30, 1975, North Vietnamese tanks entered Saigon, ending the war. The city was renamed Ho Chi Minh City, in honor of North Vietnam's charismatic leader.

THREE MILE ISLAND

THE CHINA SYNDROME, a cautionary anti-nuclear thriller, opened in theaters in March 1979. Just two weeks later the power plant at Three Mile Island, near Harrisburg, Pa., suffered the worst commercial nuclear accident in U.S. history. A sudden, silent series of critical failures deep inside Unit No. 2 was followed by conflicting reports of danger and the evacuation of some 50,000 people amid fear of the plant's invisible emissions. After six frightening days, engineers managed to control the situation, with no fatalities and no radiation poisoning. The near catastrophe—short of a complete meltdown, but more than "just a couple of chest X rays," as the head of another power company claimed—permanently changed public opinion about nuclear power.

WATCHING THE DETECTIVES

Crime-time sleuths kept bad guys on their toes

COLUMBO

PETER FALK'S Lt. Columbo used guile to ensnare his murder suspects. More resembling a skid-row bum than a top homicide investigator, and muttering his lines with a verbal slouch, Columbo wore a ratty trenchcoat and pretended to be a shuffling incompetent—until he exposed the killer, who was usually astonished to be found out. Following his hit '70s run, the durable gumshoe returned for new mystery movies in the late '80s and early '90s.

CANNON

WITH HIS AUTHORITATIVE voice, William Conrad's Frank Cannon sounded like a savvy detective—but he sure didn't look like one. The corpulent private eye, who made even Columbo look glamorous, preferred cases that paid fat fees, and lived the high life when not chasing crooks.

KOJAK

BALD WAS BEAUTIFUL when Telly Savalas played Everyman inspector Theo Kojak, a New York City policeman with a weakness for lollipops and snappy retorts. Though his catchphrase, "Who loves ya, baby?" became a classic '70s soundbite, the maverick behavior of the streetwise cop sometimes left the show open to charges of excessive violence. Even so, many police officials praised its realism.

McCLOUD

PLAYING THE CLASSIC fish out of water, *Gunsmoke* vet Dennis Weaver walked tall as Sam McCloud, a New Mexico marshal on assignment in Manhattan. With his western garb and corny utterances, the down-home lawman generally outfoxed them city slickers.

POLICE WOMAN

AS PORTRAYED by siren Angie Dickinson, Sgt. Suzanne "Pepper" Anderson brought a new dimension to the term "leg work." Her undercover duties on the LAPD vice squad allowed Pepper to assume a variety of identities, including prostitute and Mob moll, that delighted male viewers.

HAWAII FIVE-O

PLAYED BY THE always well-coiffed Jack Lord, humorless cop Steve McGarrett was oblivious to the beauty of Hawaii, where the show filmed all of its 12-season run. "Book 'em, Danno," the trademark command to his assistant, meant a bad guy was out of action.

SCARY MONSTERS

In a period bedeviled by grim news, we turned for escape—to horror

STEPHEN KING

"I THINK TERROR can be one of man's finest feelings," said writer Stephen King, who did his darnedest to scare the pants off people. In the early '70s, he taught high school English in Hampden, Maine, living in a trailer with his family. His fortunes soared after the success of his first book, *Carrie,* which hls wlfe, Tabitha, had rescucd from the trash. *Salem's Lot ,* his next, pushed his total sales to 3 million—that's a lot of fine feelings. Still tinglin' spines, in 2000 he became the first major author to publish a novel only in digital form on the Web.

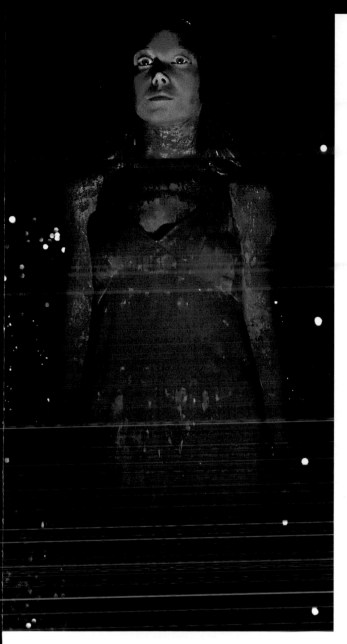

CARRIE

DIRECTOR BRIAN DE PALMA'S 1976 screen adaptation of the Stephen King novel was a bloody huge hit. The tale of a misunderstood, telekinetic teen who exacts revenge on her tormentors at the prom, *Carrie* made a major star of lead actress Sissy Spacek. Among her victims: a villainous John Travolta, then appearing on the sitcom *Welcome Back, Kotter.*

THE EXORCIST

THIS HORRIFIC 1973 story of demonic possession turned enough heads to scare up $82 million at the box office. The shocker starred young Linda Blair as the dazed-and-confused Regan, forced to play host to the ill-mannered spirit Pazuzu. In 1977, *Exorcist II: The Heretic* committed Hollywood's ultimate sin: It bombed at the box office and killed the franchise.

HALLOWEEN

SHE WAS THE daughter of movie royalty (Tony Curtis and Janet Leigh), so it was appropriate that newcomer Jamie Lee Curtis became Hollywood's princess of horror after debuting in this 1978 low-budget, high-intensity classic, directed by John Carpenter. A good turn by creepy screen vet Donald Pleasence helped make viewers' skin crawl. Soon a franchise was crawling: six sequels followed, including 1998's *Halloween H$_2$0 : 20 Years Later.*

Roots

Black Americans
unearthed their
heritage to find
pain—and pride

Alex Haley's Epic Journey

It was a staggering undertaking: For 12 years, Alex Haley devoted his time to researching and writing the story of seven generations of his family, dating back to 1750 and the enslavement of West African tribesman Kunta Kinte. The labor of love entailed visits to three continents, 6,500 hours in 57 libraries, and visits to tribal historians in remote Gambian villages. Its product—*Roots: The Saga of an American*

HISTORY LESSON
Actor LeVar Burton starred on the small screen as young slave Kunta Kinte in *Roots*.

Alex Haley returned to Kunta Kinte's Gambian village following the huge success of *Roots*, which transfixed Americans of all origins.

book melded fact and fiction—he called it "faction"—Haley was subject to increasingly harsh charges of historical inaccuracy in the high-profile months following the miniseries. Even more damaging to Haley's image, he was sued for copyright infringement by Margaret Walker, author of the novel *Jubilee*, though the case was dismissed in 1978.

If there were doubts about Haley's originality, there was no questioning his ability to tell a story. As a child in Henning, Tennessee, he was fascinated by his grandmother's tales of their slave ancestors, remembering, "When telling about Kunta Kinte, her voice would fill with awe, like she was talking about a Bible story." In the Coast Guard, Haley discovered his own gift for language, ghostwriting love letters to his shipmates' girlfriends. Later, as a freelance writer, he applied that same talent to *The Autobiography of Malcolm X,* still regarded as a landmark in African-American letters.

Broadcast rights to *Roots* were a hot property—they were sold before the book was even published. Still, ABC could not have foreseen the phenomenal success of the miniseries (followed in 1979 by *Roots: The Next Generations*). In fact, the network scheduled *Roots* for eight consecutive nights to make sure it would be over quickly in case nobody watched. Instead, the strong one-two punch of Haley's book and the TV adaptation became a cultural milestone, reaffirming the African-American experience, offering whites new insight into the black struggle, and sparking an interest in genealogy among people of all races.

Roots changed Haley's life, not entirely for the better. Though the hardcover edition had sold nearly 2 million by mid-1977, he already resented the pressures of being a celebrity. "You find that the people who celebrate you will kill you," he complained, noting wistfully, "I'd like to be famous one day a month."

Family—became a best-selling sensation after its publication in 1976. The eight-part TV miniseries based on the book, which aired on ABC in early 1977, had an even greater impact, attracting an estimated 130 million viewers.

According to Haley, the burden of *Roots* nearly proved his undoing. Sailing home from Africa during his research, deep in debt and overwhelmed by his project, the author briefly considered drowning himself—until the voices of dead ancestors urged him to continue on his mission. "I thought I was going crazy," Haley recalled. "I went back to my cabin and cried paroxysms of tears."

That flair for the dramatic may also have given ammunition to Haley's numerous detractors. Though he always acknowledged that his

Toni Morrison A born storyteller spread her wings

"IT WAS JUST a way of filling up the hours that were untaken with anything else," said Toni Morrison, recalling how she started writing. What began as a way to stave off loneliness eventually made this divorced editor one of the most acclaimed authors of the decade. Riding the same wave of interest in black history that greeted *Roots,* Morrison's 1977 novel *Song of Solomon* was a lyrical tribute to four generations of one family. The powerfully poetic work gave the literary world an unforgettable folk hero in Solomon the Flying African ("O-o-o-o-o-o Solomon done fly"), and became a main selection of the Book-of-the-Month Club, the first black novel to be so honored since Richard Wright's *Native Son* in 1940.

It was a long climb to the top for Morrison, who was born in 1931 into an impoverished but close-knit family in Lorain, Ohio. After nearly a decade of teaching, primarily at Howard University, she became an editor at Random House, working with such prominent African-Americans as Muhammad Ali and Angela Davis. Eventually taking up the pen herself, Morrison first enjoyed success with *The Bluest Eye* (1970) and *Sula* (1973), which was nominated for a National Book Award, before *Solomon* made headlines.

Morrison's stature continued to grow. Her 1987 novel, *Beloved,* captured a Pulitzer Prize, and in 1993 she became the first African-American woman to receive a Nobel Prize for Literature.

SONG SUNG BLACK "I'm never satisfied," said novelist Toni Morrison—but she brought satisfaction to critics and readers alike with her breakthrough novel *Song of Solomon* in 1977.

Muhammad

Ali's Rumble in the Jungle

A champion came back— to Africa and to greatness

FAVORITE SON "I belong to the world," said the dashiki-clad pilgrim, who proved he still belonged in the ring with his 1974 victory in Zaïre.

ON THE EVE of his October 1974 fight with George Foreman in Kinshasa, Zaïre—the "Rumble in the Jungle"—the one-time heavyweight champ looked like old news. Though he'd won a bitter, four-year legal battle when the Supreme Court overturned his conviction for draft evasion, Ali had recently been humbled in the ring. He'd lost to slugger Joe Frazier in 1971, and in 1973 Ken Norton broke Ali's jaw, proving the charismatic icon a mere mortal.

What a difference a fight makes: In the eighth round, Ali (who later admitted even he was astonished) sent Foreman packing. Delighted African fans stormed the ring, bowling Ali over. Back home, he reconsidered his decision to retire, saying, "This year has been the happiest of my life."

Other triumphs lay ahead, including 1975's "Thrilla in Manila," when Ali beat his old nemesis, Frazier. But the champ stayed in the ring too long: He was a shadow of his former self when he took off the gloves for good early in the '80s. Suffering from Parkinson's disease, Ali is now revered even by those who once reviled his politics. As his trembling fingers lit the Olympic flame in Atlanta in 1996, he proved he's still got the whole world in his hands.

HER MASSIVE AFRO and occasional pipe lent Angela Davis an air of revolution mixed with the academic. Born in 1944, Davis became a controversial civil rights militant and an outspoken Communist Party member. Alhough she studied Marxist philosophy as a graduate student, Davis told PEOPLE, "I don't have the right to lift myself out of the struggle and go bury myself in libraries or class-rooms." Her revolutionary oratory haunted her when she was implicated in a 1968 murder. In a subsequent trial that showcased her upraised fist, Davis was acquitted in 1972 by an all-white jury. She later became a prominent lecturer and writer, and was awarded a Soviet peace prize in 1979. By then her appearance, if not her views, had become less militant. Of her new close-cropped 'do, Davis told PEOPLE, "I just got tired of having to fix all that hair."

Angela Davis

Jesse Jackson

"JESSE JETSTREAM," his critics called him, for he turned up at every trouble spot around the world. The civil rights activist, Baptist minister, sometime presidential candidate and head of the Rainbow Coalition was born into poor circumstances. He was at Dr. Martin Luther King Jr.'s side when King was assassinated in 1968. Making Chicago his base, Jackson became more political in the '70s, challeng-ing the party's delegate slates at the 1972 Democratic convention. The controversial, charismatic leader later became involved in international causes, from apartheid in South Africa to Palestinian rights in the Middle East. Always, he was noted for poetic pronouncements, as in his response to President Jimmy Carter's 1979 "malaise" speech, "We've got to stop crying and start sweating, stop talking and start walking, stop cursing and start praying."

Voices of Pride
Griots with brio gave us sermons and songs

BLIND SINCE BIRTH, Steveland Morris was called the "12 Year Old Genius" when he caught the public's ear with the exuberant 1963 hit "Fingertips Part 2." By the early '70s, Wonder had wrested creative control of his work from the notoriously domineering Motown Records. Writing, producing and providing most of the voices and instruments, he created a fresh take on soul music that made inventive use of the Synclavier, an early electronic keyboard. Hits seemed to issue effortlessly—among them "Superstition" and "Higher Ground"—while albums like *Talking Book* and *Innervisions* became the era's optimistic soundtrack. Months after a near fatal 1974 car crash, the irrepressible star was back on tour, cheering his countless fans—black and white. The man who preached "survival through love" proved he was a master of both.

Stevie Wonder

Bob Marley

REGGAE MUSIC without Bob Marley? Hard to imagine. From the rubbery, hypnotic rhythms to the radical political sentiments and his striking dreadlocks, he was a one-man cultural revolution. Born in 1945 in Jamaica, Marley gained a sense of mission with his late-'60s conversion to Rastafarianism and its devotion to marijuana. Bob Marley and the Wailers became hip in America with such '70s albums as *Natty Dread* and *Catch a Fire,* and got a boost from Eric Clapton's hit cover of "I Shot the Sheriff." Addressing fears that songs like "Burning and Looting" might spark violence, Marley said, "We only want to burn capitalistic illusions." Though he succumbed to cancer in May 1980—at only 35—Marley's music still helps you lively up yourself.

FIELD OF DREAMS Paul Winfield (left) played a desperate father sent to jail for stealing to feed his family.

Sounder An encounter with poor blacks enriched us all

AMID THE SPATE of flashy "blaxpoitation" films like *Shaft* and *Superfly* that tickled audiences in the early '70s, the poignant 1972 feature *Sounder* offered a gentler, less sensational view of African-American culture. "Love and devotion … is what it is all about. This is the real black experience," reflected the movie's star, Paul Winfield.

Based on a novel by William Armstrong, *Sounder* followed the struggles of a sharecropping family in rural Depression-era Louisiana whose father was sent to jail for stealing food to feed his children. Like Winfield, co-star Cicely Tyson saw the film's strong characters as an antidote to the pimps and

MOTHER COURAGE Cicely Tyson, on left, soared as the family's matriarch.

gangsters who often populated Hollywood's movies about black life. Tyson said she had gone without work for three years rather than accept the stereotypical roles as prostitute or servant girl that were offered to her.

Winfield would later complain that because *Sounder* was made by whites—including veteran director Martin Ritt (*Norma Rae*)—the movie was not everything it could have been. But audiences and critics didn't agree. *Variety* raved that it "transcends space, race, age and time." The sentiment was reflected in the drama's four Oscar nominations, including Best Picture—though it lost to *The Godfather*. Tyson and Winfield reunited in 1977's similarly inspiring modern-day tale *A Hero Ain't Nothin' but a Sandwich*.

Black Comedy
Finally, dark stars started shining in TV's white world

The Jeffersons

A SPINOFF of *All in the Family,* this series starred Sherman Hemsley as blowhard George Jefferson, former neighbor of Archie Bunker, and Isabel Sanford as his sensible wife, Louise. The Jeffersons struck it rich in the dry-cleaning business and left working-class Queens for a classy Manhattan high-rise, proving the American Dream still exists—at least in sitcoms. The show's theme, "Movin' on Up," captured its optimism.

Sanford and Son

REDD FOXX was blue: The comedian was notorious for the vulgarity of his stand-up routines. But he cleaned up his act in this hit sitcom from top '70s producer Norman Lear. Adapted from a British series, the comedy starred Foxx as Fred, a rascally Los Angeles junk dealer, and Demond Wilson as his thirtyish son Lamont, who was often dismayed by his dad's antics. The series ranked among TV's Top 10 shows in its five-year run.

Flip Wilson

"THE DEVIL made me do it!" was Wilson's excuse, and audiences were glad he did: For its first two seasons, *The Flip Wilson Show* placed second in the ratings, an unprecedented feat for a black variety series. The show featured music and guests, but the fans really flipped for Wilson. Among the versatile comic's characters were the swinging and spunky Geraldine Jones (above), the sleazy Rev. LeRoy, private detective Danny Danger, and Herbie, the Good Time Ice Cream Man.

SANFORD AND SON SALVAGE WE BUY AND SELL JUNK

JUST FOR SHOW?
Any quiet moments in
the stormy relationship
of Elizabeth Taylor and
Richard Burton seem
to have been as staged
as this '72 photo shoot.

love
american style

From palimony to the Pill, the '70s remade romance

liz taylor

Leaving Burton's house, she wound up with a Senator

The year is 1977: A 45-year-old woman is dishing up turkey in a Virginia school when a student puts a sanitary hairnet on her head and dubs her an honorary cafeteria maid. It's not exactly an Oscar, but

EQUINE AND DINE Liz and John toured his country estate in 1977. They exchanged vows on a hillside at the farm in '76.

Elizabeth Taylor already has a couple of them: right now, she's nuthin' but net. Only ... how did she get here?

BY 1970, LIZ TAYLOR, AT 38, had been a major star since she appeared in *Lassie, Come Home* at 11. The sheer arithmetic of her past was daunting. She'd had five husbands (hotelier Nicky Hilton, actor Michael Wilding, producer Michael Todd, singer Eddie Fisher, actor Richard Burton). She'd won two Oscars (*Butterfield 8*, 1960, and *Who's Afraid of Virginia Woolf*, 1966). And she'd had one scandalous affair—with Burton, while she was still married to Fisher—on the set of *Cleopatra* (1963).

Liz married Burton in 1964, and the couple embarked on a boozy, self-destructive decade that spawned memorable headlines—and mostly forgettable films. Tired of his drinking and wandering eye, Taylor divorced Burton in 1974. But after diverting herself with former used-car dealer Henry Wynberg, Liz

BACK TOGETHER Reunited, Liz and Dick posed in 1975. He told PEOPLE: "We really cannot keep away from each other."

remarried Burton in October 1975. No luck: they divorced again in 1976.

That was America's Bicentennial summer, and the man in charge of the celebration was John Warner, a stalwart Republican from a patrician Washington, D.C., family who liked to play nature's nobleman on his 1,000-acre farm. The year before, he had been set up as Taylor's date to a function for another regal Liz—Queen Elizabeth II—and sparks had flown.

Liz and John married in December 1976. As he eyed his ultimately successful bid to become Senator from Virginia, Liz gamely worked the cafeteria circuit with him. "I'm very happy and contented being out to pasture as the wife of a country squire," she told PEOPLE, adding, with a wink: "He's the best lover I've ever had." Maybe so—but in 1982, she'd wash that man right out of her hairnet, and send him on his way.

ryan & ali
The decade set sail on a tide of tears

HERE'S THE PITCH: Preppy, smart rich boy meets poor, smart Italian girl. His tyrannical father opposes the match. They get married anyway, and then the girl gets sick and dies. The story sounds stale thus stripped to its bones, but when 33-year-old Yale classics teacher Erich Segal skillfully updated Juliet and Romeo, and Hollywood put them on the screen in the form of Ali MacGraw and Ryan O'Neal— it was soon raining Kleenex in the theater aisles. *Love Story* was *the* monster smash of 1970-71, with the novel topping the bestseller charts and the movie packing theaters.

One reason for the film's success was the welcome fantasy of its premise: *Love Story* was a harbinger of the new decade's trek from political to personal concerns. Though set on Boston college campuses at the height of the '60s, the tearjerker featured two clean-cut kids who didn't smoke dope, didn't protest the war and were polite to their dads. Only in Hollywood!

Love Story made MacGraw and Ryan white-hot. The Wellesley-educated MacGraw was a former model who had starred in 1969's *Goodbye, Columbus*—and just happened to be dating *Love Story* producer Robert Evans (they later wed). O'Neal went on to star in 1973's *Paper Moon* (with Oscar-snagging daughter Tatum) and 1975's *Barry Lyndon*—and to spend many years linked with another icon of the '70s, Farrah Fawcett.

LOOT STORY Critics called it trite, but huge crowds gave the film the largest opening weekend in Hollywood history to date. It took in a whopping $2,463,916— more than it cost to make. (Ticket price: $3.)

paul & joanne

Hollywood's happiest couple lived in Connecticut

"I AM LURCHING TOWARD 50," Paul Newman told PEOPLE in 1974, "with all the eager anticipation of a kid having a woman for the first time." Well, nice try, Paul, but we can't believe you savored aging that much, even if you did look 35 then, not 49. One thing we believe, though: wherever Newman was going, he'd get there fast. When not making movies (he'd already earned Oscar nominations for *Cat on a Hot Tin Roof, The Hustler, Hud* and *Cool Hand Luke*), his favorite haunt was the inside of a race car. A buff since he starred as a driver in the '69 film *Winning,* Newman joined a Ferrari team at the Bonneville Speedway in Utah in October '74 as it aimed to beat the world land-speed mark (he topped 200 m.p.h., but not the record).

The secret to Paul's verve? His marriage to the gifted actress Joanne Woodward—and their three children—kept Mr. Blue Eyes grounded, as did the couple's decision to skip the Hollywood madness and put down their roots in a leafy Connecticut town, Westport.

"T" FOR TWO Who's that on Joanne's T-shirt in this 1974 shot? Why, it's none other than her sometime director, co-star and husband since 1958—you know, the guy on the right.

jimmy & rosalynn

Y'all come! A laid-back President and First Lady made their House a home

AFTER LONG YEARS of what some called the "imperial presidency," Jimmy Carter and his wife Rosalynn came to the White House in 1977 determined to restore the common touch to the executive mansion. Carter was an Annapolis graduate who had put his Navy uniform in mothballs to take over his family's peanut business in the small town of Plains, Ga. A deeply religious man, Carter entered politics, became governor, then swept into the presidency in 1976, thanks to Watergate-weary voters.

The Carters traced their relationship back to childhood. Jimmy's sister Ruth had been Rosalynn's best friend. His mother,

Lillian, a nurse, had attended Rosalynn's father during his fatal battle with leukemia.

After a double date when Jimmy was a midshipman, he told his mother, "She's the girl I want to marry." Carter proposed; Rosalynn turned him down, then relented. One score of years and four children later, the Carters moved into the White House, despite a rare gaffe on Jimmy's part: the scrupulously honest candidate told *Playboy* in an interview just before the election that "I've committed adultery in my heart many times." Rosalynn Carter, a good Baptist, forgave his low-down fantasies. Just imagine ... lust in the White House!

SET A SPELL The Carters kick back in their new digs in '77. Aiming to downsize the presidency, they rationed *Hail to the Chief*. As Baptists, they banned hard liquor from the premises.

woody & diane

Witty, smart and with-it, they made neuroses trendy

PUTTIN' ON THE RITZ: For him, it involved a wimpy rain hat pulled down tight, a nebbish's slouch and a mournful countenance; for her, perhaps a man's tie or vest and rummage-sale slacks. But when Woody Allen and Diane Keaton went out on the town, they packed all the style they needed in their hyperactive brains and well-developed funny bones. For one brief, shining moment in the mid-'70s, they reigned on America's movie screens as the king and queen of urban cool, all angst and complexes and self-lacerating put-downs.

Brooklyn-born Woody first achieved fame as a gag writer and stand-up comic, then as the force behind such zany cult films as *Bananas*. Keaton came up in the theater, even playing a role in *Hair* on Broadway (though she was too self-conscious to strip in the nude scene). Though they broke up as lovers in 1972, when they reunited as actors to bring their giddy improv style to film in 1975's *Love and Death* and 1977's *Annie Hall*, the result was—la-de-dah—screen bliss.

HAT TRICK The ditzy duo in '72. Diane was Woody's third love. An early marriage to Harlene Rosen lasted six years, and he broke up with his second wife, actress Louise Lasser, after five years.

GOOD DEAL **The happy couple in the mid-'70s. Inventorying his recreational habits for PEOPLE in '75, Jack said he smoked pot, "occasionally" snorted coke and had dropped "a good deal" of acid.**

jack & anjelica

Hollywood's hot duo flew too close to the flame

JACK NICHOLSON'S wayward eyebrows and shark's grin kicked around Hollywood for years until they made him a star in 1969's *Easy Rider*. But from beginning (*Five Easy Pieces,* '70) to middle (*Chinatown,* '74) to end (*The Shining,* '80), Jack *owned* the '70s, winning the Best Actor Oscar for *One Flew Over the Cuckoo's Nest* in 1975.

Married to actress Sandra Knight for four years in the 1960s, Nicholson later linked up with model Mimi Machu and singer Michelle Phillips. But his great love for most of the 1970s was Anjelica Huston, 24 in 1975, the daughter of legendary movie director John Huston (who played *Chinatown*'s incestuous villain).

Huston was an aspiring actress, but after a few roles in 1969, she vanished from the screen. It was not until she teamed up with Jack on film, in the 1985 black comedy *Prizzi's Honor* (director: John Huston), that she flashed the sly wit and dark beauty that would make her an enduring star. The couple stayed together until 1992.

In 1977 Nicholson and Huston were caught up in a sordid story from L.A.'s fast lane: *Chinatown* director Roman Polanski pleaded guilty to having sex with a 13-year-old girl at Nicholson's Bel Air home. The actor wasn't present; it was Huston who walked in on the two. In the subsequent search, she was arrested for cocaine possession; the charges were dropped when she agreed to testify against Polanski.

sleeping around

They took a spin on the '70s' merriest go-round

shampoo

WHAT A STRETCH: Warren Beatty played a hairdresser whose customers keep saying "'do me!" in this 1975 comedy of manners. The film sought to capture the feel of Hollywood in the late '60s. But in doing so, it reflected (and exploited) the new sexual frankness that was taking over mainstream America in the '70s. Beatty was no summer soldier in this revolution: His '70s consorts included Michelle Phillips and one *Shampoo* co-star: Julie Christie, left—not Goldie Hawn.

WHEN THE three rocking Britons in Fleetwood Mac invited Americans Stevie Nicks and Lindsey Buckingham to join them, the result was musical magic—but bedtime bedlam. Let's see: First drummer Mick Fleetwood's six-year marriage soured. Then singer Christine McVie and bassist John McVie ended their seven-year marriage, and she took up with Beach Boy Dennis Wilson. Then Stevie and Lindsey, a couple for eight years, went their own ways. So she took up with ... Mick.

fleetwood mac

last tango in paris

PERHAPS WE should have called this entry "Love American/ French/Italian Style." Directed by Bernardo Bertolucci, *Last Tango* starred a multinational cast speaking both French and English. But who was listening? Here were Marlon Brando and Maria Schneider—embracing, stripping, coupling with a raw edge main-stream audiences had never seen before. The film opened the flood-gates for a tide of sexy movies. And it gave Brando, 48 when it was released, one of his last great screen roles.

lee & michele

No vows? No problem: She sued for "palimony"

HE WAS THE GRIZZLED tough guy of *The Man Who Shot Liberty Valance* and TV's *M Squad;* she was a blues singer trying to forge a career in Hollywood. Their 1964 meeting wasn't cute—it was on the set of the gloomy flick *Ship of Fools.* Both were in flight from failed marriages: Lee Marvin's 12 years with wife Betty had produced four children, but little joy. Michele

Triola had just divorced actor Skip Ward. So when they moved in together, they skipped the "I dos."

Michele later claimed she gave up her own career as she helped Marvin's thrive in *The Dirty Dozen* and *Cat Ballou.* Then, in 1970, Marvin hurriedly married an old flame—and his lawyers asked Michele to leave his Malibu home (he sent her $800 a month for 18

months). Scorned, Michele hired lawyer Marvin Mitchelson to sue Marvin in 1972, pioneering a new kind of suit—not for alimony, but "palimony." In 1979, Michele was awarded $104,000, far less than the $1.8 million she'd sued for. Vindicated, Michele laughed last: "I'm ready for marriage now," said she. Nope! Still unmarried, she is now Dick Van Dyke's best pal.

HAPPY DAYS Lee and Michele posed at a mid-'60s Hollywood hobnob. Ironically, after she filed suit, the notoriety made Marvin a more bankable star.

They helped every gal of a certain age feel younger

burt & dinah

FOR A FEW years after he first swaggered onto the movie screen in 1972's *Deliverance*, Burt Reynolds was the star some women hated to love. His persona hovered a bit too close for comfort to the good-ol'-boy roles he played in movies like *White Lightning* (1973). Some missed the joke when he posed for *Cosmo*, stripped to his hairpiece. His marriage to *Laugh-In*'s Judy Carne didn't last.

But then Burt did something that made him the toast of women everywhere: he fell in love with the gracious, mint-julep-voiced singer from Tennessee, Dinah Shore—who, at 57, was 19 years his senior. Dinah had been a famous songbird since the early '40s, while Burt was one of Hollywood's biggest male stars. They met in 1971 when Burt was a guest on Dinah's TV talk show. "I liked her immediately," Burt told PEOPLE in 1974. "I fell in *like*."

Soon enough, it was love, if not marriage. Dinah's 19-year marriage to actor George Montgomery had ended in divorce, as had a one-year match with a Palm Springs contractor: Burt later said "neither of us mentioned the M-word." The Burt and Dinah show lasted for four happy years, ending in 1975. Though Burt moved on to Sally Fields, he and Dinah stayed close: In 1979, four years after they split, Dinah visited Burt's parents in Florida twice. Now, that's class.

DECEMBER AND MAY
Burt's first turn on her talk show, Dinah said, was so randy it took two hours of taping to come out with 15 minutes that weren't "X-rated."

TOP GUNS The Muppets were omnipresent in the late '70s, from their first movie to their TV series to their key role on the PBS hit *Sesame Street*.

miss piggy & Kermit

THE MOST ROMANTIC MOVIE STARS of 1979 were a pig and a frog: When Miss Piggy and Kermit hit the big screen in *The Muppet Movie*, their tale of sheer animal passion became one of the nation's biggest films, even as their series *The Muppet Show* was a hit on TV. Yet tragedy lurked behind the triumph: "Miss Piggy doesn't have the greatest body or the greatest voice," said Muppetman Frank Oz, who enjoyed a close relationship with the porcine star, even as he kept her at arm's length. "So there's been rejection. But underneath the glamor and the bravado she's very courageous."

Affable Kermit vowed to keep his webbed feet firmly on the ground, despite his success. "There are two openings in life for a frog," he told PEOPLE through his personal manager, Muppet boss Jim Henson. "He can go into show business— or he can wind up on a plate. It isn't easy being green."

She wrote her name on his heart in indelible oink

ling-ling & hsing-hsing

They charmed humans but flopped at the birds 'n' bees

PAGING BOB DOLE: For many years after they arrived in Washington, D.C.'s National Zoo as gifts from China, America's favorite (and, at the time, only) giant pandas made a botch of their annual roll in the bamboo. Ling-Ling, the female, and Hsing-Hsing, the male, couldn't seem to get into the swing-swing. Unstudly Hsing-Hsing appeared to be stuck in an adolescent fumbling stage. "He's kind of poking around, but can't find the right spot," said the zoo's curator for the pandas, Bill Xanten. The missus seemed to find the whole business fatiguing, if not downright demeaning, and often flopped to earth at the critical moment.

The pandas were given to America as a goodwill gift by Mao Zedong to mark President Richard Nixon's landmark 1972 visit to Beijing. The National Zoo spent $500,000 for fancy digs for the roly-poly pair, and the debut of the couple stirred up nationwide panda-monium.

Finally, the pandas produced five full-term cubs, all of which died shortly after birth, victims of insufficient immune systems. Ling-Ling died in 1992, at 23, a venerable age for her kind. Hsing-Hsing lived on alone, dying in 1999 at age 27. There were no survivors.

ALL TEASIN', NO PLEASIN' Chinese experts recommended that the plump pandas (here in 1981) be put on a diet. But even slimmed down to a svelte 275, they still didn't mate for years.

odd couples
We loved these preposterous pairs

oscar & felix

THEY WERE THE THIRD DUO to play the slobby sportswriter and his uptight roomie, but Jack Klugman and Tony Randall are the ones we remember. (The prior pairs were Walter Matthau and Art Carney in Neil Simon's Broadway hit, and Matthau and Jack Lemmon in the 1968 movie.) In 1997 the eternally youthful Randall, then 77, fathered a baby girl with his 26-year-old wife, Heather Harlin.

laverne & shirley

TALK ABOUT THE THEORY of relativity: this spinoff from *Happy Days* starred Penny Marshall, wife of Rob Reiner, a.k.a. "Meathead," Archie Bunker's son-in-law. Penny's brother Garry was the show's co-creator and executive producer; her dad was producer. Within a year, Penny (Laverne) and Cindy Williams (Shirley) had TV's No. 1 show. Marshall, who split from Reiner in 1981, also had played a recurring role on *The Odd Couple;* she's now the director of hits like *A League of Their Own.*

mork & mindy

ROBIN WILLIAMS wasn't really an alien—he just played one on TV. An unknown when the series started in 1978, Williams, then 26, beguiled viewers as "Mork from Ork." His secret: "I pick up a verbal shotgun and go berserk. Otherwise you end up giving in to TV." When the brilliant onetime Juilliard student took control of your TV, it seemed less predictable than ever before. Though his first marriage didn't last and he dabbled in drugs in the '80s, Robin would become a major movie star. Pam Dawber (Mindy) married actor Mark Harmon in 1987 and continues to act.

the newlywed

mick & bianca

WHEN YOU'RE rock's premier sex symbol, your fans expect you to tie the knot in style. So … champagne bottle? Check. Half-smoked joint? Check. New wife's breast partially exposed? Check. All was in order on that day in Saint Tropez, France, in May, 1971, when Mick Jagger was finally snagged by Nicaraguan beauty Bianca Perez Morena de Macias. Satisfaction? Well, the marriage ended in 1980.

MOVIE STAR GRACE KELLY hated her 1956 wedding to Prince Rainier of Monaco: she felt it had been a garish spectacle. So when her daughter Caroline, 21, married Philippe Junot, 38, in 1978, the vows were private, though the newlyweds did promenade through the tiny principality's streets. There were rumors that the bride's parents didn't trust Philippe, a ladies' man and unabashed bon vivant whose source of income was unclear. The marriage ended after two years.

caroline & philippe

game

BRITONS HADN'T cheered a royal wedding since Queen Elizabeth's sister, Princess Margaret, married Anthony Armstrong-Jones in 1960. So when Elizabeth's only daughter, Princess Anne, wed Captain Mark Phillips, a commoner, in 1973, the British people pumped up the pomp. Though Anne and Mark shared a love of horses and had two children, Peter and Zara, they parted in 1989; she wed Naval officer Timothy Laurence in 1992.

anne & mark

tricia & ed

AMERICANS HAVE ENJOYED only eight White House weddings: The most famous was the 1906 marriage of Teddy Roosevelt's daughter Alice to congressman Nicholas Longworth. So it was a special day in June 1971, when Richard Nixon escorted daughter Tricia to her Rose Garden wedding to Ed Cox, a New York City lawyer. (Special guest: Alice Roosevelt Longworth, age 87.) Still together, they have one son, Christopher.

COOCHIE COOCHIE
Born in Spain in 1945, Maria Rosario Pilar Martinez Molina Baeza adopted a farcical Castilian accent and skin-tight clothing to reinvent herself as Charo—or, to be more precise, Charo!

WHAT WERE WE THINKING?

Nightmarish clothes, improbable celebrities and unlikely fads made the '70s wacky, tacky and wonderful

CHARO!

We fell for the act of this manic Hispanic

TAKE ONE PART GRACIE ALLEN, one part Mamie Van Doren and one part Ed Sullivan's mouse-marionette Topo Gigio. Blend thoroughly and *presto*—Charo! The young bride of bandleader Xavier Cugat, Charo had a gift for fracturing English—and filling out a sexy costume—that made her the perfect "entertainment" on countless Bob Hope specials. The truth: Her ditziness was a superb act, for Charo was smart and gifted. Trained by Andres Segovia, she was a fine guitarist—and was fluent in Japanese. She retreated to Hawaii in the '80s and eased into semi-retirement secure in this boast: She'd made more appearances on TV's *The Love Boat* than any other guest star.

SUSAN ANTON

SHE WAS GOING TO BE the next big thing. The stunning six-footer and former Miss California went from TV-pitchwoman-as-sex-goddess (Muriel cigars, Serta mattresses) to one-hit movie wonder (she was the robotic super-athlete "Gold-engirl" in the 1979 film of the same name) to star of some very bad TV specials. The irony: Anton was not only gorgeous but also engaging and intelligent—and we wanted only to look at her.

SHAUN CASSIDY

HE WASN'T DYNAMIC like his Broadway-actor father, Jack. He wasn't blessed with the vocal gifts of his mother, musical-comedy star Shirley Jones. But it seemed his destiny to be famous. And so he was—first as a soft rocker, then as a TV heartthrob (starring in *The Hardy Boys Mysteries* from 1977 to 1979). Though an attempted transition to hard rock would come to naught, when Cassidy was hot, prepubescent girls swooned. But—as they always do—they grew up. Shaun kept his head and went on to a successful career as a TV producer.

THE BAY CITY ROLLERS

THE NEW BEATLES? That's how their manager touted them. Still, their tartans were cute, and for a moment in 1975, courtesy of their hit single "Saturday Night," Rollermania ruled. But the group's fall from the pinnacle was steep: later years brought members' suicide attempts and arrests for indecency; Roller Billy Lyall died from AIDS in 1989. The first pop group to emerge from Scotland, the Rollers got their name when mentor Tam Paton purportedly stuck a pin in a U.S. map and hit Bay City, Mich.—the hometown of the *next* decade's megastar, Madonna. No, we don't make this stuff up.

BILLY CARTER

IN 1977, with personal appearances and endorsements, he earned half a million dollars—two and a half times the salary of his brother, the President. The peanut farmer from Plains, Ga.—the good ol' boy with the REDNECK POWER bumper sticker on his pickup—was the "other" Carter, and never more so than when he lent his name to "Billy Beer."

THE GONG SHOW

TO CALL IT AMATEURISH was to miss the point, for rough edges were the stock in trade of this Dadaist game show. It debuted in 1976 with its creator, game-show king Chuck Barris, as master of revels. A celebrity panel was subjected to, and sounded the dreaded gong for, a ragtag crew of bizarre talents, whose acts made Charo look sophisticated. Upon the show's demise, Barris retreated to France. (Well, the French do love Jerry Lewis.)

Yesterday's trash—is today's trash too

THE LAVA LAMP

IT HARNESSED CHEMISTRY to create pseudo-psychedelic imagery. The Lava Lamp's 40-watt bulb heated a goo of clear liquid and buoyant, colored wax. The result: stretching, slithering amoebas of color. First launched in the '60s, it was still trippy in the '70s. Now—they're back!

THE PET ROCK

THINK OF IT as the Hula Hoop of the '70s—so silly you had to love it. And while it may have been stupid, it landed the fad's creator, California ad man Gary Dahl (above), on *The Tonight Show* twice. The novelty was the stocking stuffer of choice for Christmas 1975—a marketing whim dreamed up the previous April by Dahl and his buddies as they sat around bemoaning the chores that arrive with "real" pets. The beauty was in the details: All pet rocks came with detailed instructions for caring for, and training, your inert, boxed buddy.

THE MOOD RING

ONLY A SELF-ABSORBED DECADE could have given us a fad based on the idea that the world was interested in your mood at all times. Wall Street dropout Josh Reynolds (left) came up with the idea of jewelry featuring heat-sensitive liquid crystals that changed color according to body temperature. Blue meant blissful; black was a bummer. Everybody wore one: Dustin, Barbra, Cher, even Muhammad Ali. Tens of thousands sold, from $5 knockoffs on the street to $250 14-karat gold models from Bonwits. Then … the mood passed.

JONATHAN LIVINGSTON SEAGULL

AUTHOR RICHARD BACH'S spiritual parable about a seagull in search of self-discovery, fulfillment and a higher meaning to his life—beyond pecking for food, that is—struck cynics as bird doo. But the slight 1970 book, with "inspirational" photos by Russell Munson, gulled enough readers to become a self-help classic.

CB RADIO

IT BEGAN as a way for lonely, long-haul truckers to stay in touch. But suddenly citizens' band radios went mainstream, and it seemed everybody got in on the act. When even housewives had handles like "Wacky Witch" and "Night Owl," and CB lingo ("Breaker breaker, good buddy!") became a national fad, it was clearly time for a pop anthem. Enter Nebraskan Bill Fries (above), who, as C.W. McCall, wrote and recorded the 1975 country crossover hit "Convoy." By 1979 there were 14.3 million CB licenses. That's a big 10-4.

fashion went from mod to mortifying

SYNTHETIC SYMPHONY

WOMEN'S STYLES are often flamboyant. But in the '70s, men (for once) followed suit. Check out swimming hunk Mark Spitz, outshining wife Suzy Weiner in a two-toned, pinstriped, vested tux. Ow!

A STARRING ROLE in *Pretty Baby* (1978) put Brooke Shields in the news—and in the company of cool cat Jimmy McNichol, whose Travolta look is lifted verbatim from *Saturday Night Fever.*

DENIMIC DUO

FEW NAILED the '70s blend of lame and fame quite as well as siblings Donny and Marie Osmond, whose variety show ran on ABC for four seasons beginning in 1974. Trend setters? Absolutely not. But when the denim bandwagon rolled by— turning prole '60s gear into pricey '70s high style—the Osmonds jumped on in a big way, along with designers such as Calvin Klein and Gloria Vanderbilt. The western-inspired denim-with-appliqué look was huge, if a little cornpone. And hey, Donny, isn't the turquoise-and-silver necklace a bit busy?

TOO HOT TO COOL

THE FAILURE of the fashion gurus to force women into matronly "midi" skirts, some said, helped swing the fashion pendulum the other way—and gave us hot pants. The term was coined by *Women's Wear Daily* in 1971 to describe the shockingly tarty short-shorts that began to be sported that year, even by sweet Mary Tyler Moore (who's cheating by wearing dark panty hose underneath). Maximum exposure and freedom of movement for dancing made hot pants ideal disco wear. But it was celebs like Marlo Thomas, Jackie Onassis and, yes, Liz Taylor, who helped bring the bare-up-to-there look to your local mall.

BOUNCIN' & BEHAVIN' HAIR

TAILOR MADE for spinning, "the wedge" was popularized by Olympic gold medal figure skater (Innsbruck, 1976) Dorothy Hamill. Women stormed salons nationwide to get the high-style, low-maintenance cut.

ARTFUL FEATHERING, extra-large rollers and close-to-the-scalp teasing were the keys to turning Farrah Fawcett's dishwater-blond tresses into the sexy, tousled 'do that became a classic in the annals of '70s hair. Jennifer, give me that blow dryer, right now!

BLAKE EDWARDS'S 1979 film *10* made Bo Derek into the decade's last sex symbol. Who could resist her great crossover style—a white girl with braided, beaded cornrows—running in slow motion to Ravel's "Bolero"?

DISCO INFERNO

From the big screen to the radio to the dance floor, a seductive new style ignited the night and transformed our culture

"Disco sucks!" was the cry of out-raged rock and rollers, but we just couldn't resist the big-beat dance craze—not after we got our first glimpse of John Travolta's moves in that Trojan horse of the disco army, 1977's all-conquering *Saturday Night Fever.* Originally the province of gays and blacks,

John Travolta

FEVER PITCH "I wouldn't know what it's like not to be an icon," said John Travolta, who proclaimed early on his intention to become a respected actor, the Robert De Niro or Al Pacino of his generation.

THE RIGHT MOVES
Travolta trained three months to prepare for the dance sequences in *Saturday Night Fever.* Style tip: The pants and shirt were sewn together to keep his shirttails from coming loose.

disco's pounding beat had rug cutters of all ages doing the hustle after *Fever* ran its course: both its star and its Bee Gees-driven soundtrack won over the masses.

"As a kid, I was a seductive brat," recalled John Travolta, who began to insinuate himself into our hearts from his first days on TV. As dim Vinnie Barbarino, he helped make *Welcome Back, Kotter* a sitcom smash in 1975. The next year, he played the title role in the TV-movie *The Boy in the Plastic Bubble,* co-starring with Diana Hyland, who became his first love (despite being 18 years his senior). He was a memorable bully in '76's feature fright fest *Carrie.*

As *Fever*'s Tony Manero, the troubled Brooklyn teen who comes alive strutting his stuff on the disco floor in a white suit, Travolta electrified audiences with a mixture of arrogance and vulnerability. Critics slammed the movie's melodramatic plot, but even the most jaded observers found Travolta and his piercing blue eyes irresistible. *The New Yorker* observed, "He seems incapable of a false

note." But John's triumph was tinged with tragedy: In the midst of filming, Diana Hyland succumbed to cancer, dying in his arms.

Fever became a phenomenon, grossing $74 million in the U.S. alone, and bringing Travolta an Oscar nomination. The soundtrack sold 30 million copies, setting a record, while discos sprouted across the country. Even on vacation in Tahiti, Travolta was mobbed by teenagers chanting, "Disco king!"

After *Fever,* Travolta's career was more mercurial than a thermometer. He soared again in *Grease* and looked cool in *Urban Cowboy,* but he faded in the late '80s, resorting to *Look Who's Talking* in 1989. Married to actress Kelly Preston in 1991 (and now the father of two), the longtime Scientologist came back strong in '94's *Pulp Fiction,* earning a second Oscar nomination. "It never occurred to me that my career wasn't salvageable," said Travolta, Tony Manero-style.

The Bee Gees

The Brothers Gibb cloaked sex in satin

THEY WERE HAS-BEENS by the early '70s: After a string of Beatles-esque '60s hits that included "To Love Somebody," the Bee Gees had split up, reunited and come back with the '71 sob story "How Can You Mend a Broken Heart?" Then the public tuned out. So Barry Gibb and his younger, nonidentical twin brothers Robin and Maurice reinvented themselves. Hitching their fortunes to the disco craze, they blended shrill falsetto harmonies with funky tempos on smashes like 1976's

"You Should Be Dancing." That was just a warm-up. Dominating the soundtrack of *Saturday Night Fever,* they caught fire with three straight No. 1 singles: "How Deep Is Your Love," "Stayin' Alive, and "Night Fever." The Gibbs also wrote and produced hits for others, among them Frankie Valli ("Grease"), younger brother Andy Gibb (who passed away in 1988) and even Barbra Streisand. Although the Bee Gees cooled as disco faded, they continue to record, minus those booming beats.

GEE WHIZ
"We want to go out on top," said Robin (center), who hit the high notes with Barry (left) and Maurice in this' 79 gig.

STARS OF THE MIRROR BALL

Their flash, flesh and flair made us feel like dancin'

The Village People

COWBOY, INDIAN, cop, hard hat, soldier and biker: The Village People played manly stereotypes to the hilt. The creation of French producer Jacques Morali, who was inspired by dancers at Greenwich Village gay clubs, the guys represented disco at its most cartoonish and exuberant, scoring thumping hits like "Macho Man" (1978) and "Y.M.C.A." (1979). Their cheesy flop movie *Can't Stop the Music* was hardly prophetic: In 1981 they morphed into a "New Romantic" act, then faded from sight. Now they're back as an oldies act: Thousands of very straight Americans join forces with them to scream "Y.M.C.A."—once a gay anthem.

Patti LaBelle

A VETERAN of the '60s R&B scene, Patti LaBelle (center) resurfaced as leader of the silver lamé-clad Labelle, which also featured Nona Hendryx (left) and Sarah Dash. Their tasty 1975 chart topper "Lady Marmalade" glorified the street walker's life with its hilarious come-on: *"Voulez-vous couchez avec moi ce soir?"* Ooh la la!

Donna Summer

COOING, SIGHING and moaning with unmistakable intent, Donna Summer simulated the sounds of passion on her 17-minute orgasmathon, "Love to Love You Baby" (1975). The sultry singer enjoyed a longer run than most disco acts, scoring hits like "I Feel Love" and "Bad Girls." After becoming a born-again Christian in the '80s, Summer alienated fans with apparently homophobic remarks; she pleaded not guilty.

KC & The Sunshine Band

BOOGIE MAN Harry Casey (far right) brought a breezy tropical slant to his party tunes, topping the charts with such infectious no-brainers as "That's the Way (I Like It)" and "(Shake, Shake, Shake) Shake Your Booty." Just when his "Miami Nice" sound seemed to be out of gas, KC rebounded with a change-of-pace ballad "Please Don't Go." Play that funky music, white boy!

ON THE OUTS Studio owner Steve Rubell, trying to keep the "gray people" at bay, was assaulted when he told one man, "You're ugly, I don't want you here."

Studio 54

Sex, drugs 'n' disco fueled a notorious celebrity playpen

THE MOTHER of all disco clubs, Studio 54 carefully screened its guests when it opened in a former TV studio on Manhattan's 54th Street in 1976. Co-owners Steve Rubell and Ian Schrager sought just the right crowd mix: Rubell called it "tossing the perfect salad." Outside, mobs of hopefuls pressed against the velvet ropes guarded by bouncers. Inside, 54 was a thundering hothouse where beautiful people danced, chattered, scored drugs, hit on one another—and scoped out the basement VIP room. *Everyone* came: President Carter's elderly mother, Miz Lillian, said after her visit, "I don't know if I was in heaven or hell. But it was *wonderful*." In 1979 the two owners were convicted of tax evasion and both served prison terms. Rubell died of AIDS in 1989; Schrager is now a family man and hotel mogul. Under new ownership, Studio 54 closed as a disco in 1986. It has since served as a home for rock concerts and plays.

STUDIO 54 PHOTOGRAPHS BY ROBIN PLATZER

CABARET LIFE A shining, silky Liza Minnelli, then an accomplished party-goer, showed off her dance technique and dazzling smile for friends and strangers alike at the hedonistic hangout.

MUSICAL CHAIRS **Rocker Rod Stewart, Alana Hamilton (a.k.a. Mrs. George Hamilton, who became Mrs. Stewart in '79) and Yankees fan Elton John surveyed the sizzling scene.**

HOME CLUB **Ballet great Rudolf Nureyev and dancing mate Sterling St. Jacques got down and flirty in '79 on the party pad's put-upon parquet.**

VERY FUNNY **Gilda Radner, cute in overalls, yapped it up with Ernest Hemingway's widow Mary and his glamorous granddaughter Margaux.**

The Scene At Studio 54

I GOT YOU, BABE Cher, post-Sonny, mid-Gregg and apparently in a John Denver state of mind, got down on 54's dance floor with screen-writer pal Howard Himmelstein.

WHAT A BORE! High-profile owner Steve Rubell, left, hung with Mikhail Baryshnikov and a jaded Mick Jagger at Bianca Jagger's birthday fling in '77.

Celebrities with little in common but renown were 54's drawing card. From left, designer Halston, jet-setter Bianca Jagger, Jack Haley Jr. and his missus at the time, Liza Minnelli, cozy up to Jermaine Jackson.

WALK
ON THE
WILD
SIDE

Pied Pipers of excess flourished in an age of extravagant display

DAVID BOWIE

He mixed up rock, art, space and sex in his gender-bender blender

THE MAKEUP, THE MYSTERY, the studied androgyny, the bisexuality: The whole bizarro package threatened to obscure the music. Almost. But David Bowie's otherworldly sounds entranced us—who could resist his invitation to "turn and face the strange"? He was always ahead of his time: "Space Oddity" was released in 1969, but didn't click until reissued in '72. By then, Bowie's persona had merged with Ziggy Stardust, the title character of his '72 hit album. (The ultimate superstar, Ziggy was prisoner to the adulation he inspired.) He was unforgettable onstage, strutting in a dyed-red brush cut and a signature eye patch—covering, insiders knew, a paralyzed pupil, the result of surgery following a schoolyard scuffle. The patch was an emblem of the performer's duality: Beneath the glitter and glam lurked an ambitious former commercial artist named David Jones. Director Nicolas Roeg's oblique film *The Man Who Fell to Earth* (1976) nailed Bowie's image as a melancholy innocent, a decidedly unisex alien, searching for utopia and love among the stars. But Bowie, like John Lennon, hated labels—"Changes" was his anthem—and other personas, like the Thin White Duke, soon appeared. Finally he chose to come down to earth; he's been happily married to supermodel Iman since 1992.

ALL GUISE, NO DOLLS Bowie, here in 1978, commanded stages with an eerie, compelling mastery. As much a thespian as a rock star, he proved a brilliant shaper of his own image, onstage and off. "I am an actor," he once said. "My whole professional life is an act. I slip from one guise to another, very easily."

EVEL KNIEVEL

A cowboy cyclist sold us a **vroom** with a view

SURVIVING A ROUSTABOUT boyhood in his native Butte, Mont.—he was a hubcap stealer and all-around hell-raiser—Robert Craig Knievel flirted with trouble for years. He claimed he was a card sharp, con man and safecracker. In 1965 he invented his own occupation: Professional Risk Taker. A hog-ridin' fool, "Evel" wondered how far a guy on two wheels could leap through the air—and how much people would pay to see him do it. The result: a career of heart-stopping stunt jumps that amazed audiences from Las Vegas to London. At Wembley Stadium in May 1975, Knievel successfully cleared 13 double-decker buses, though he broke his pelvis by crash-landing. No problem: Five months later, he made it over 14 Greyhound buses at Ohio's King's Island amusement park—while setting an *ABC Wide World of Sports* viewership record. "I know someday someone may outjump me," Knievel once said. "But they will never out-promote me." Think again, Evel: Today your gutsy son Robbie is out to do both—and he may just die trying.

ANDY WARHOL

He took fame's picture—and turned it into art

ANDY WARHOL'S FAMOUS remark—"In the future, everyone will be world-famous for 15 minutes"—seems true about everybody but its author. He just goes on and on, long after his untimely death from a heart attack in 1987 (after undergoing routine gallbladder surgery). Visionary? Fake? Social climber? Genius? Our final answer: Warhol would no doubt embrace all these labels. After growing up in a "Czech ghetto" outside Pittsburgh, he split for New York, where he became a pioneer of Pop Art and an explorer of alternative lifestyles. In 1968 he was shot by a crazed female fan; afterward, he seemed more devoted to decoding fame than creating art. In the '70s his *Interview* magazine wallowed in celebrity, publishing verbatim transcripts of dishy gossip with Liza, Halston, Mick and Bianca as it obsessively covered Manhattan's nighttime demi-monde of the hip and the hangers-on. A lionizer of trivial subcultures? Arguably. An insightful chronicler of an age fixated upon the image? Definitely.

STARS OF A DIFFERENT STRIPE Warhol waxed patriotic with "superstars" Jane Forth, left, and Ultra Violet, in 1970.

ROCKET MAN **Knievel was 34 when, on Sept. 8, 1974, he climbed into this jet-powered gizmo and tried to make a one-mile jump across the Snake River Canyon in Idaho, some 2,500 feet above ground. But his parachute opened too soon, and Evel suffered a rare fizzle. We loved him anyway.**

A subversive band of comics liberated the boob tube from its play-it-safe formulas

TWO-TIMERS The second-year cast of "Not Ready for Prime Time Players," from left: Garrett Morris, John Belushi, Jane Curtin, Laraine Newman, Bill Murray, Gilda Radner and Dan Aykroyd. Murray replaced first-year-only cast member Chevy Chase. The show debuted at 11:30 p.m. on Oct. 11, 1975—a time slot it has held ever since.

SURE, WE'D SEEN stuff as smart as it was funny on TV before: Think *Laugh-In* or The Smothers Brothers. But not this smart, this funny—or this live. In the pre-cable era, network-TV viewing choices were limited to bland and blander. *Saturday Night Live* put an end to that, exploding onto screens with comedy that dared to skewer politics, drugs, sex, even TV's most sacred moments—the commercials. Canadian-born producer Lorne Michaels, the brains behind the show, had recruited a cast of edgy, brash comics, many of them—John Belushi, Dan Aykroyd, Gilda Radner—from the famous improv group, Second City. Soon every kid in America was mouthing *SNL*'s catchphrases: "Jane, you ignorant slut" … "We are two wild-and-crazy guys" … "I'm Chevy Chase and you're not."

That first season, each of the players made less than $1,000 a week—but that would change as the show became a celebrity machine, making mega-stars of many of its cast members. And though critics carp that the now 25-year-old show never again reached the daring originality of its early years, *SNL* remains a breeding ground for our best comic talent. If you don't agree … well, in the immortal words of John Belushi, as an immigrant learning English: "I would like to feed your fingertips to the wolverines."

ALIENS The Coneheads hailed from Remulac, which, they maintained, was "a small town in France."

NOOGIES Bill Murray's nerdy Todd DiLaMuca got fresh with Gilda Radner's adenoidal Lisa Loopner.

PATTY HEARST

EXTRA! Newspaper heiress now gun-totin' rebel!

THE GENTEEL BERKELEY co-ed was dragged screaming from her apartment by kidnappers on Feb. 4, 1974. When she reappeared at the Hibernia Bank in San Francisco's Sunset District two months later, she was the rifle-bearing terrorist Tania—foot soldier in a cadre of left-wing wackos, the Symbionese Liberation Army—who dissed her own family as "the pig Hearsts." For Tania was Patricia Campbell Hearst, the granddaughter of legendary newspaper mogul William Randolph Hearst. It took 20 months for the FBI to track her down: Nabbed, she claimed she had succumbed to starvation and brainwashing. At her trial for armed robbery, the jury showed no mercy and sentenced her to seven years. But she served less than two before President Jimmy Carter granted her clemency. Bringing her strange saga full circle, Hearst married her former bodyguard, San Francisco policeman Bernard Shaw, in 1979. Moving east, she began life anew as a conservative housewife and mother—and occasional bit player in the offbeat films of director John Waters.

REBEL, REBEL Hearst, as Tania, posed as an SLA cadet in '74.

HAPPY ENDING Patty and Shaw honeymooned in Panama.

RICHARD PRYOR

He got under our skin—by telling the truth

HE WAS HIGH-VOLTAGE. Intense. A crude, shrewd, hilarious dude. Deeply race-conscious at times, he was willfully color-blind at others—but always at his best when forcing Americans of all stripes to confront their racial hang-ups. Richard Pryor had the right lineage to become America's down-and-dirtiest comic: His grandfather owned a pool hall in Peoria, Ill.; his grandmother ran a bordello; and his mother was a prostitute who married the madam's son. Pryor turned it all into laughter through characters like Mudbone, an ornery black preacher, and Lightnin' Bug Johnson, a sweet wino. He also earned three Grammys and an Oscar nomination for his role as the junkie Piano Man in 1972's *Lady Sings the Blues*.

Sadly, self-destructiveness was more than a role for Pryor. As Bill Cosby once said, "For Richard, the line between comedy and tragedy is as fine as you can paint it." Badly burned freebasing cocaine in 1980, Pryor recovered and beat his drug problems—but since 1986 he has suffered gravely from the effects of multiple sclerosis.

TESTIFYING Pryor performed in California in 1978. He mixed brutally frank sexuality, mercilessly harsh language and voices from a seamy childhood to outrage his audience. But his point was never simply to offend: it was to confront painful realities and provoke thought. In Pryor's hands, comedy became a kind of shock therapy.

A CLOCKWORK ORANGE

THE TAGLINE OF Stanley Kubrick's 1971 film said it all: "Being the adventures of a young man whose principal interests are rape, ultraviolence, and Beethoven." It wasn't for everybody. Based on the novel by Anthony Burgess set in a vaguely futuristic Britain, the movie is stylized to the hilt and disquieting in the extreme. Gangs of teenagers—"droogs," led by Alex, played by a young and charismatic Malcolm McDowell—go on nightly murderous rampages ("a bit of the old ultraviolence"). Jailed by the police, Alex volunteers for "aversion therapy" to cure himself of hooliganism – and a grotesque morality play of sorts begins. Kubrick himself described the film as a meditation on whether, deprived of the choice between good and evil, we can retain our humanity. After its release, the movie spurred copycat crimes in Britain, and Kubrick withdrew it from theaters there.

DEEP THROAT

IN THE YEARS since the groundbreaking, 62-minute film's release, the phrase has come to evoke Watergate more than sex. But after its 1972 release, *Deep Throat* scandalized America: Its wholly unexpected mainstream popularity was a death knell for the clear line that separated "clean" from "dirty" movies. Catapulting actress Linda Lovelace (born Linda Boreman) to worldwide notoriety, the film is said to have grossed (the correct term, to many) perhaps half a billion dollars.

Porn movies had always been with us—so why was *Deep Throat* such a breakout success? First, it had strong production values. It was shot on 35mm film in Eastmancolor—several cuts above the grainy, black-and-white level of run-of-the-mill porn. Second, it caught just the right wave, appearing at a time when Americans were in the throes of the sexual revolution, discarding old boundaries like last year's fashions. Third, it offered an imaginative plot conceit: Its central character is a woman whose clitoris is located in her throat—with obvious implications. But the film's "fun," its star claimed in her 1980 book, *Ordeal,* belied the horror of its making. Linda said she had been a virtual prisoner to her sadist husband at the time, who used violence to force her to participate in the porn industry.

GERARD DAMIANO'S

DEEP THROAT

HOW FAR DOES A GIRL HAVE TO GO TO UNTANGLE HER TINGLE?

EASTMANCOLOR Ⓧ ADULTS ONLY

LENNY

IT WAS AN UNEXPECTED pairing, but it worked: Song-and-dance man Bob Fosse directed this gritty, powerful 1974 homage to the pioneering '60s comic Lenny Bruce. Self-destructive and brilliant, Bruce became the most controversial comedian of his time with a hip, abrasive act that focused on left-wing politics and was laced with four-letter words. Fosse's film took the form of an interview-style biography, with star Dustin Hoffman's Oscar-nominated performance baring Bruce's drug problems with unblinking realism.

THE ROCKY HORROR PICTURE SHOW

DECADES AFTER its 1975 release, it's still filling midnight shows with the form its fans invented: The audience is part of the show, and that means reciting the script verbatim, dressing in costume and bringing your own props. A hilarious spoof of both sci-fi and horror flicks, set to a rock-and-roll soundtrack, *TRHPS* tells the story of Brad and Janet (Barry Bostwick and Susan Sarandon), strictly white-bread honeymooners from Denton, Ohio, who get a flat tire and stumble upon the castle of transvestite mad-scientist Dr. Frank N. Furter—a cross-dresser from another galaxy—played with leering, lascivious glee by Tim Curry. Wonderfully silly and surprisingly multilayered, the film struck a chord, first with the hip crowd, then the general public. Fans boast they've seen it hundreds of times, always finding something new: Hey—isn't that Meat Loaf as "Eddie"?

LOOKING FOR MR. GOODBAR

WHOLESOME STAR Diane Keaton struck many as a strange choice to play the lead in director Richard Brooks' 1977 film of the urban horror classic by Judith Rossner. Keaton played a proto-typical '70s character: Theresa Dunn, a teacher of deaf children by day—and a sexually adventurous denizen of singles bars by night. But Keaton's nuanced performance was acclaimed, as was the film, as much for its realistic take on many Americans' new sexual mores as for the sheer terror of its ending.

Goodbar—which was the first movie to depict recreational drug use as many Americans practiced it—featured Richard Gere in an electrifying turn as the male hustler Tony that put him on the fast track to stardom. Controversial when it was released, *Goodbar* accurately reflected (and exploited) America's rapidly changing moral landscape.

ROUGE 'N' ROLL

Acting up, acting out (and sometimes just plain acting), musicians made a spectacle of themselves

ALICE COOPER

TUBES OF MASCARA accompanied him on tour; parading around with a boa constrictor was just one trick in his bag—a guillotine was another. It was all part of Vince Furnier's role as Alice Cooper, lead singer of what he called "the sickest, most degenerate rock band in America" (Are you listening, 14-year-old boys?). Beneath the makeup, this proto–Marilyn Manson was a normal guy, born in middle-class circumstances and raised in Phoenix. What he lacked in musical ability or originality, his group made up for in extremes of silliness and drama—but both the band and its fans were in on the joke. After the group's popularity peaked in 1972 with the million-selling single "School's Out," Cooper's penchant for beer led to a much-publicized drinking problem. But Furnier hushed up his telltale vice: The master of Grand Guignol loved to play golf.

QUEEN

THEATRICALITY? Queen owned the concept in rock, with concerts that featured sepulchral white smoke, enormous costs for lighting effects ($250,000 on one tour), a 5,000-pound "Crown of Yesteryear" that levitated from the stage as if by magic—and, not least, the group's flashy vocalist and leader, Freddie Mercury (who was born Frederick Bulsara in Zanzibar). With ingenious arrangements that managed to straddle the border between glam rock and heavy metal, Queen's Brian May, John Deacon and Roger Taylor, along with Mercury, below, hit the Top 10 in the U.S. with "Bohemian Rhapsody" in 1976. The hit showcased the group's tight harmonies and May's virtuoso guitar work, which would drive such future smashes as "We Are the Champions" and "We Will Rock You." Sadly, Mercury—a fine writer and born showman—succumbed to AIDS in 1991.

KISS

IN CONCERT, they vomited blood and spit fire. They took sudden, airborne flights across the stage. They wore makeup reminiscent of a kabuki troupe performing *Cats.* And they were airport-runway loud. These shock rockers, who first broke through in '74, were a parent's worst nightmare—particularly vocalist/bassist Gene Simmons and his infamous, serpent-like tongue. Was it any wonder that a Holiday Inn in West Virginia refused to house the group? No matter: Their young fans ate it up. Simmons (left), Paul Stanley (center), Ace Frehley (right) and Peter Criss (on drums), offered rebellion in a very safe package. There was even a Kiss cartoon show on Saturday-morning TV. To their fans' delight, the graying geezers are still on the road and still spittin' blood.

THE SEX PISTOLS

THE SPICE GIRLS of their day? 'Fraid so—these heralds of punk were working-class Britkids carefully packaged by canny manager/promoter Malcolm McLaren. Leaders Johnny Rotten, right, and Sid Vicious, left, brought a studied nastiness (and proud amateurism) to the stage, as black-lipsticked, spiky-haired, safety-pin-clad fans reveled in their nihilism and raw style. Vicious, in over his head, died of a heroin overdose in 1979.

PHOTO CREDITS

COVERS Front: Travolta: Michael Childers/Corbis Sygma; clockwise from top right: Bruce McBroom/MPTV, Kobal Collection (2), ©1978 Bregman-Sutton/MPTV, Tony Costa, NBC/Globe, Ron Galella/Ron Galella Ltd., Everett Collection. **Back:** Douglas Kirkland/Corbis Sygma

TITLE PAGE/CONTENTS i Tony Costa ii Robin Platzer/Twin Images, Bob Scott/Neal Peters, NBC, MPTV, Harry Langdon/Shooting Star iii Fred Maroon, Ron Galella/Ron Galella Ltd., Michael Montfort/Shooting Star, Bob Adelman/Magnum

THE WAY WE WERE 1 NBC/Globe 2 Everett Collection 3 John Zimmerman/Time Inc. 4 ABC/Neal Peters Collection 5 Globe 6-7 Photofest 8-9 AP/Wide World

THE ME DECADE 10 Dick Luria/FPG 11 ©1978 Gunther/MPTV 12 ©1990 Bob Gruen/Star File 13 David Hume Kennerly/The White House 14 Don Ornitz/Globe, Michael Ochs Archive 15 Amalie R. Rothschild/Star File, Michael Ochs Archive, Martin Mills/Shooting Star 16 Michael Dobo, Steve Hansen 17 Thomas Victor, Ken Regan/Camera 5, Shooting Star

SINGULAR SENSATIONS 19 Kobal Collection 20 Phil Roach/IPOL 21 Robin Platzer/Twin Images, Ken Regan/Camera 5, Phil Roach/IPOL 22 Ron Galella/Ron Galella Ltd. 23 Liaison 24 Globe 25 Michael Putland/Retna, Kobal Collection 26 ©1978 Gene Trindle/MPTV, no credit 27 John Engstead/MPTV, Steve Schapiro 28 Everett Collection 29 Robin Platzer/Twin Images 30 David Gahr, ©1978 Lynn Goldsmith 31 Kobal Collection 32 Alan Pappe 33 Burt Glinn/Magnum 34 Ken Regan/Camera 5 35 RB/Redferns/Retna, Andrew Kent/Retna 36 S. Karen Epstein 37 Fin Costello/Redferns/Retna, Tom Zimberhoff/Contact 38 Vivlota/The Image Bank, Brenda Piekutowski/Neal Peters 39 Ken Duncan 40 Fotofantasies 41 Kobal Collection, Universal Pictures/Shooting Star 42 Kobal Collection 43 Bruce McBroom/MPTV, Photofest 44 UPI/Corbis Bettmann 45 Co Rentmeester/LIFE, Heinz Kluetmeier/SPORTS ILLUSTRATED

I AM WOMAN 47 David Redfern/Retna 48 Corbis Bettmann 49 A.E. Woolley/Globe 50 Tony Korody/Corbis Sygma 52 Ken Regan/Camera 5 53 Ron Galella/Ron Galella Ltd.

AMERICAN PIE 55 Globe 56 Ron Galella/Ron Galella Ltd. 57 M. Childers/Corbis Sygma 58 Everett Collection 59 NBC/Neal Peters Collection 60 Alan Pappe/Neal Peters 61 ©1973 Universal/MPTV, ©1978 David Sutton/MPTV 62 Jeff Mayer/Star File, Michael Putland/Retna 63 Larry Dale Gordon/Corbis Sygma, Ken Regan/Camera 5 64 John Olson/LIFE, Raeanne Rubenstein, Globe 65 Ted Streshinsky, no credit, Al Freni

DARK SIDE OF THE MOON 67 Globe 68 UPI/Corbis Bettmann 69 Edie Baskin/Corbis Outline 70 Dirck Halstead, Steve Northup, Fred Maroon, UPI/Corbis Bettmann 71 UPI/Corbis Bettmann, no credit, Alfred Eisenstaedt/LIFE, Steve Northup, Corbis Bettmann 72 Mary Ellen Mark/Mary Ellen Mark Library 73 Everett Collection 74 Corbis Sygma, Alain Mingam/Liaison 75 John Paul Filo, UPI/Corbis Bettmann, J.L. Atlan/Corbis Sygma 76 Photofest, Everett Collection 77 Kobal Collection, Lester Glassner Collection/Neal Peters, CBS/Neal Peters Collection, Everett Collection 78 Tom Jones 79 Photofest, Kobal Collection, ©1978 Falcon International/MPTV

ROOTS 81 no credit 82 Michael Mauney 83 Yale Joel/LIFE 84 Howard Bingham 86 Adrian Boot/Retna, Jeff Mayer/Star File 87 Ken Regan/Camera 5, Richard Mellou/Corbis Sygma 88 Kobal Collection (2) 89 Everett Collection, NBC/Neal Peters Collection (2)

LOVE AMERICAN STYLE 91 Liaison 92 IPOL Archive/IPOL, Robert Penn/Corbis Sygma 93 Photofest 94 ©2000 Archives of Milton H. Greene, LLC www.archivesmhg.com 95 Dennis Brack/Black Star 96 Ron Galella/Ron Galella Ltd. 97 Phil Roach/IPOL 98 Everett Collection 99 Neal Preston/Corbis, no credit 100 Globe 101 Globe 102 Henson Associates 103 National Zoological Park, Washington, D.C. 104 Everett Collection, ABC/Neal Peters Collection 105 Kobal Collection 106 Patrick Lichfield/Camera Press/Retna, Melloul/Corbis Sygma 107 Hulton Getty/Liaison, Co Rentmeester/LIFE

WHAT WERE WE THINKING 108 ©1978 Wallace Seawell/MPTV 110 Yoran Kahana/Shooting Star, Steve Schapiro/Corbis Sygma 111 Paul Schmulbach/Globe, Everett Collection, Leviton-Atlanta 112 Frank White, Al Freni, James A. McInnis 113 John Olson/LIFE, Leviton-Atlanta, Jim Collison, no credit 114 NBC/Globe, Phil Roach/IPOL, Robin Platzer/Twin Images 115 Phil Roach/IPOL, Shooting Star, Tony Triolo/SPORTS ILLUSTRATED, no credit, Orion/Neal Peters Collection

DISCO INFERNO 117 Douglas Kirkland/Corbis Sygma 118 Kobal Collection 119 Allan S. Adler/IPOL 120 Lynn Goldsmith/Corbis 121 E. Biebl/Shooting Star, G. Hannekroot/Retna, Jeffrey Mayer/Star File 122-125 Robin Platzer/Twin Images (9)

WALK ON THE WILD SIDE 127 Michael Putland/Retna 128 Gianfranco Gorgoni/Corbis Sygma 129 Everett Collection 130 Photofest 131 NBC/Neal Peters Collection (2) 132 no credit, Phil Roach/IPOL 133 Ace Burgess/Globe 134 Everett Collection, Neal Peters Collection 135 Fox/Neal Peters Collection, Kobal Collection (2) 136 Richard E. Aaron/Corbis Sygma, Jeff Mayer/Star File 137 Bob Gruen/Star File, Lynn Goldsmith/Corbis